KINSHIP AND COMMUNITY IN
TWO CHINESE VILLAGES

BURTON PASTERNAK

Kinship & Community in Two Chinese Villages

STANFORD UNIVERSITY PRESS

Stanford, California 1972

Stanford University Press
Stanford, California
© 1972 by the Board of Trustees of the
Leland Stanford Junior University
Printed in the United States of America
ISBN 0-8047-0823-1
LC 72-78870

TO A ROSE

Preface

WHEN I went to Tatieh it was with the intention of gathering data for a general ethnographic account of a reasonably "traditional" Chinese village under the impact of Land Reform. I selected Tatieh village in particular because it was located in the Hakka region of south Taiwan and everyone assured me that the Hakka were unquestionably "the most conservative Chinese" on Taiwan. Not only was Tatieh discrete spatially, but it gave all indications of being a socially integrated community as well. It was large enough to promise an opportunity to observe a full round of community life, but it was not so large as to preclude the development of personal familiarity with all inhabitants. Tatieh was also far enough from a major industrial-urban complex to reduce the likelihood of massive disruption from that source. Finally, I had good contacts in Tatieh and adequate housing was available for one ethnographer and his very pregnant wife—with room for expansion.

As it turned out, Tatieh was the right place for other reasons. As the data accumulated, it became clear that this community departed in significant ways from my mental image of a "traditional" Chinese rural setting, and I eventually came to focus on certain peculiarities in an attempt to account for them. It was a desire to further explore and elaborate hypotheses formulated in Tatieh that led me, a few years after that, to settle down in Chungshe.

Chungshe village promised to provide an opportunity to contrast a reasonably "traditional" Hokkien community with a Hakka one. The two villages were quite similar physically, demographically, and in terms of proximity to an urban-industrial center. My earlier work in Tatieh had stimulated my interest in the social correlates of irrigation technology. Recent irrigation modifications in Chungshe were quite opposite to those in Tatieh and I was very interested in determining whether or not the social consequences of these modifications would turn out to be predictably different. Initial inquiries suggested other differences of interest between the two communities. Lineages were apparently better developed than they had been in Tatieh, and inter-ethnic fighting did not appear to have been nearly so important a phenomenon in this area. Again, I was assured of basic accommodations in Chungshe for myself, my wife, and, by that time, our two children.

Fieldwork in Tatieh (January 1964 to June 1965) was funded by the Foreign Area Fellowship Program. Research in Chungshe (May 1968 to June 1969) was conducted under a grant from the National Science Foundation. I am most grateful for the generous support provided by both of these agencies. Although they made this book possible, neither of them should be held accountable for its defects. A list of all the individuals who have helped and encouraged me at various points along the way to completion of this manuscript would be longer than any publisher, no matter how softhearted, could possibly be expected to allow. But special thanks are due to T. H. Liu, Steven Lai, Paul Chiu, Thomas Chien, and Y. K. Tsung, who guided and assisted me during the fieldwork phases of this project; and to the people of Tatieh and Chungshe, who most generously and patiently endured my "big nose" in their private affairs as well as my incredible ignorance regarding things that every normal person ought to know. Then I must thank my colleagues Dan Gross, Mel Ember, Carol Ember, Mervin Meggitt, and Myron Cohen. Although all of these people contributed valuable suggestions on how I might improve upon earlier versions of this book, they are not in any sense responsible for the shortcomings of the present version.

Finally I reserve a very special expression of gratitude for my wife, Brigitte, who held my hand, banked my fires, wiped my brow, and otherwise sustained, aided, and encouraged me at every point along the way. She contributed most generously of her intellect and ingenuity in the field, and her editorial skill was essential to the preparation of this book.

B.P.

Contents

Illustrations

Tables

KINSHIP AND COMMUNITY IN
TWO CHINESE VILLAGES

ONE

Introduction

Tatieh and Chungshe are Chinese villages. In terms of language, family, links between families, and the nature of community integration, they have much in common with other Chinese villages. Although both are inhabited by the descendants of pioneers who came to Taiwan from the southeastern Chinese mainland, their current social fabric emphasizes different elements of a common cultural inventory, with the result that life in Tatieh has a different texture and coherence from life in Chungshe. The main difference is that in Chungshe patrilineal affiliation has long played a greater role in determining the nature and form of social relations.

Tatieh, a nucleated multi-surname community, was settled about 1811 by Hakka immigrants from Kwangtung province. As a ceremonial, social, political, and economic unit it has always been highly integrated. Corporate lineages appeared early but never achieved elaborate development within the village, either structurally or in terms of the property they controlled. The development of patrilineages within Tatieh was early compromised by a variety of corporate cross-kin associations that served to integrate the community by uniting families of different kinship, class, and ethnic provenance. Nonlocalized descent groups ultimately emerged and linked agnatic groups in different Hakka communities.

Chungshe, also a nucleated multi-surname community, was founded about two hundred years ago by Hokkien-speaking peoples whose ancestors came from Fukien province. One descent group has long dominated social, political, and economic relations within the community. It is more elaborately developed than any descent group in Tatieh and more closely resembles the southeastern model of the strong, localized, corporate, patrilineal descent group described by Maurice Freedman (1958, 1966) and others (Baker 1968; Potter 1968, 1970). It is composed of corporate branches within corporate branches—a nesting pattern that is socially, ritually, and politically manifested. There is no evidence of higher-order (i.e. nonlocalized) descent groups linking Chungshe to other communities. Cross-kin associations analogous to those in Tatieh have been rare in Chungshe and have tended to mirror a variety of cleavages linked to distinctions in wealth, residence, and agnatic affiliation.

The relative stress on patrilineal affiliation in Chungshe is manifested in other ways. Marriage, more so than in Tatieh, tends to be arranged in such a way as to separate affinally related families, and family ceremonial practices generally reflect a sharper separation between affines and agnates. Sons are more likely to be adopted from families closely related by agnation than in Tatieh, and patrilineal affiliation has played a more important part in determining access to vital economic resources. Village relations and even ceremonial behavior are also more closely linked to agnatic affiliation.

It has long been recognized that Chinese do not everywhere organize themselves in precisely the same way. Less clear, however, have been the conditions under which one form of organization is likely to be favored over another. Why Chungshe villagers should be more inclined to emphasize patrilineal ties than Tatieh villagers is the subject of this book. The differences between Tatieh and Chungshe do not lend themselves to simple explanations in terms of degrees of urbanization or modernization, or in terms of ethnic provenance. They are more likely the product of certain social, geographical, and economic features peculiar to the rural setting in which each community was established and evolved. Of particular importance have been the nature of subsistence resources and the way in which access to land and irrigation water has been obtained, maintained, and defended in each case. The hypotheses that I will suggest to account for the differences between Tatieh and Chungshe may have general relevance for southeastern China. They may tell us something about conditions under which multi-lineage communities are likely to appear and about the conditions under which agnatic affiliation will be played down in such a setting. Finally, they may reveal the circumstances under which descent groups of various sorts are likely to be formed.

The remainder of this chapter is devoted to a brief description of Tatieh and Chungshe villages. In Chapters 2 through 4 we focus upon specific differences in terms of agriculture, family relations, relations beyond the family, ceremonial patterns, and village integration. In Chapter 5 we discuss a number of possible sources of variation and attempt to indicate the most probable ones. Our findings will then be projected against available materials for southeastern China to determine the extent to which our hypotheses find support.

TATIEH

Tatieh is one of seven villages in Hsinpi township, in the county (*hsien*) of Pingtung. It is located in the eastern portion of a narrow coastal plain in southwestern Taiwan (see Map 1). Pingtung city, the county seat, is 25 kilometers to the north. Nine kilometers to the east great mountain ranges rise to heights of over 2,000 meters; twelve kilometers to the west the plain meets the sea along a flat, meandering coast. The main provincial highway runs within one kilometer of the village, linking it to district and county seats and to major cities. Besides reliable bus service, villagers have access to railroad stations a few kilometers away. Bicycles, radios, and motorcycles are commonplace. Television sets are still a luxury but there are a few.

According to my survey done in 1964, the community contained a total resident population of 1,602, distributed among 265 households. The median household size was 6.0 persons. The economically least productive age categories (i.e. those under sixteen and over 60) made up 49 percent of the total population. Nuclear and

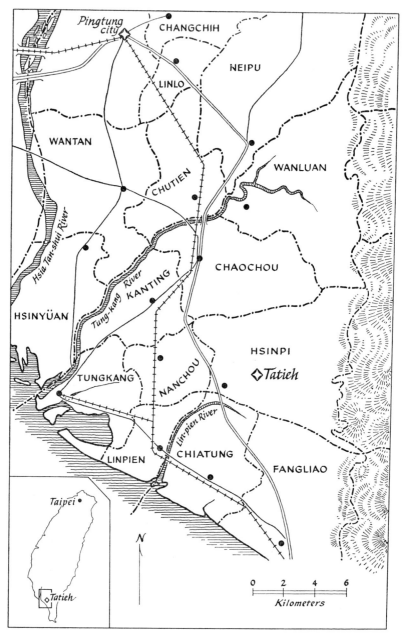

Map 1. Hsinpi and neighboring townships

stem families were predominant; 4.9 percent of all village households contained families of the joint type.[1]

At the time of my fieldwork in Tatieh (1964–65), Hakka speakers constituted over 95 percent of the village population. The rest consisted of Hokkien speakers and more recent immigrants from non-Hakka areas of the Chinese mainland. Adjacent regions to the north and west of the community are largely inhabited by Hokkien-speaking peoples. Aborigines belonging to the Paiwan group live in the mountains nearby. The area directly south of Hsinpi is mainly inhabited by Hakka.

Tatieh literally means "blacksmithing." Local legend has it that the community's first settler was a blacksmith. Members of each of the largest surname groups in the village assert historical priority in the community by claiming the legendary blacksmith as their ancestor. Twenty-nine surnames are currently represented in the village, the three most common being Liu, Hsü, and Ch'en (accounting for 13, 14, and 19 percent of all households, respectively). The remaining surnames each account for less than 10 percent of all households.

According to the Liu written genealogy, Liu Ying-p'iao was the first person of his surname to be buried in Tatieh. He was born in 1777 and died in 1851. Assuming that he was about 30 years old when he arrived in Tatieh, his descendants have been in the village for about 164 years. They now comprise 33 households (64 percent of all Liu and 13 percent of all village households). Genealogical materials for the Hsü and Ch'en families are lacking in detail. Although no dates are mentioned, the first person of each surname to have settled in Tatieh is indicated. If we assign twenty years to a generation, we can estimate that Hsü and Ch'en have been in Tatieh for about 160 years.[2] Households tracing de-

1 My use of the terms nuclear and joint is similar to that of Olga Lang (1946: 14–15). A joint family contains two or more married siblings; a nuclear family consists of a married couple and their unmarried children. My use of the term stem differs slightly from Lang's. It refers to a family larger than nuclear that does not meet the requirements of a joint family (i.e. it does not contain two or more married siblings).

2 If this method of calculation is applied in the case of the Liu, where dates are already known, we arrive at precisely the same figure (i.e. 160 years). The assignment of twenty years to a generation would therefore seem reasonable.

scent from the first Hsü settler now number 37 (95 percent of all Hsü and 14 percent of all village households). The progeny of the first Ch'en ancestor now constitute 31 households (60 percent of all Ch'en and 12 percent of all village households).

Tatieh is best described as a nucleated settlement. Small shrines at each of the four entries mark the limits of the residential area, from which fields spread out in all directions. A number of shops and stalls, strung around the main crossroads, provide villagers with most of their supplies. Itinerant merchants bring in fresh food each morning. A visitor to Tatieh is at once impressed by its relative prosperity. Streets are paved with asphalt and are well lit at night. Electricity was brought in by 1930, and all homes make use of it. Most houses are built of kiln-baked brick, often faced in concrete, and are covered with the traditional pink tile roofs. In most cases, floors are of cement. Homes and streets appear neat and orderly. The village temple, first built during the latter part of the nineteenth century, has been repaired and expanded many times over the years. It is spacious, ornate, and very well maintained. Many villagers send their preschool children to its nursery, and it is the hub of community ritual activity. A few pious men and women live there and cultivate the temple's nearby fields.

The physical distribution of homes and fields in Tatieh evidences considerable interposition according to surnames—a pattern that contrasts sharply with the oft reported tendency of Chinese to segregate themselves in terms of agnatic affiliation (see Baker 1968: 117–30; Freedman 1958: 1–3; Potter 1968: 14–22; and C. K. Yang 1959b: 11, 81).[3] But there is reason to believe that families of the same surname were once more clearly demarcated. The oldest houses belonging to each main group are located at a sizable distance along the main street. Villagers claim that immigration and population growth gradually broke this pattern and led to the more mixed residential pattern that now characterizes the community.

---

[3] Describing conditions in Nanching, for example, C. K. Yang observed that "between members of different clans there was a clear demarcation, expressed not only in the independent centers of life within each clan and the inter-clan rivalry which was alive in practically everyone's mind, but also, and visibly, in the separation of living quarters within the village grounds" (1959b: 11).

Households in Tatieh typically reside in compounds that minimally consist of a row of rooms facing a courtyard. The center room, or *cheng-t'ing*,[4] is the ancestral hall in which are kept the ancestors' spirit tablets and the representations of various deities. The *cheng-t'ing* normally doubles as a sitting room, since it is the most impressive room in the compound. Bedrooms and kitchens flank this room on both sides. As each household partitions, bedrooms and kitchens are added to this basic structure; and in the course of time the compound with its wings commonly assumes an L or U shape. The number of households that inhabit a compound is therefore signaled by the number of kitchens that it contains. Households sharing a compound are most often closely related by agnation. They may consist of the progeny of a common father, grandfather, or great-grandfather. When space does not permit further expansion, newly emerging domestic units begin a new compound, which is preferably, but not necessarily, near the old one. The households that take up residence in a new compound initially continue to worship their ancestors in the original ancestral hall. But each new compound normally is built around a *cheng-t'ing*, and after a time new ancestral tablets will be lodged there.[5] When this is done, ritual dependence upon the parent compound hall comes to an end. As we shall see, the placing of ancestral tablets in a new compound hall does not invariably lead to ritual separation in China.

In 1964, the vast majority of Tatieh's households depended on farming for their livelihood. Climate and soils in this region of Taiwan are especially suitable for cultivation. Tatieh lies within the "highest-temperature and highest-rainfall district" of Taiwan (*Soils* 1961: 59). The average annual mean temperature for the district as a whole is 76.8°F, and there is only one month during which the mean temperature drops below 68°. The average annual rainfall is 97.4 inches, most of which falls from May through September. The result of this rainfall pattern is that the region sometimes experiences an alternation between flooding and drought.

---

[4] Throughout this book Hakka and Hokkien Chinese terms are romanized in terms of their Mandarin equivalents.
[5] There is no prohibition against the duplication of ancestral tablets.

TABLE 1

Main Crops Grown in Tatieh Village in 1960

(*hectares*)

Crop	Grand total	Paddy				Upland			
		Sub-total	Winter crop	First crop	Second crop	Sub-total	Winter crop	First crop	Second crop
Paddy rice	346.70	346.70	—	174.40	172.30	—	—	—	—
Sweet potatoes	44.59	22.23	11.08	6.97	4.18	22.36	9.23	6.01	7.12
Soy-beans	47.64	43.61	42.67	.94	—	4.03	2.07	1.48	.48
Other beans	20.40	20.15	20.15	—	—	.25	.25	—	—
Sugar-cane	11.58	.57	.19	.38	—	11.01	3.64	7.01	.36
Vege-tables	16.65	12.66	2.68	4.71	5.27	3.99	.41	3.09	.49
Bananas[a]	9.47	3.58	—	—	—	5.89	—	—	—
Green manure	226.20	225.61	117.95	107.66	—	.59	.05	—	.54

SOURCE: Agricultural Census of 1960, data for Tatieh village.
  [a] Only compact plantation areas included.

Village soils are azonal in type and mainly slate alluvial in terms of parent materials. They have a silt loam surface underlain by a silt-clay loam subsoil. The clay content is not so great as to pose a problem for drainage or tillage, and Tatieh's soils are very suitable for the cultivation of rice, sugarcane, sweet potatoes, and many other crops (see Chen Cheng-siang 1963: 135–39; and *Soils* 1961: 17–19). When properly irrigated and drained, they can yield two crops of paddy rice and a winter crop of soybeans each year (see Table 1). Banana became the second most important crop in terms of acreage in 1963. Secondary crops include vegetables, fruit, peanuts, and betel nuts. Sugarcane is grown mostly by the sugar refinery on its own fields.

The total area of land cultivated by villagers has changed very little since the 1949 Land Reform Program (see Table 2).[6] The Program ultimately increased the cultivator-owned portion of

  [6] For a general review of the Land Reform Program on Taiwan, see Chang Yen-tien (1954) and Chen Cheng (1961).

TABLE 2

Ownership of Land Cultivated by Tatieh Villagers, 1952–64

Year	Cultivator-owned		Tenant-cultivated	
	Hectares	Percent	Hectares	Percent
1952	108	48%	116	52%
1960	178	82	39	18
1964	191	87	29	13

SOURCE: Figures for 1952 are based on materials in the *Hu-shui tsung t'iao-ch'a chi-lu piao* (Household tax general investigation record). The Committee on Agricultural Census of the Taiwan Provincial Government provided the figures for 1960. Those for 1964 were compiled by me. In arriving at them, comparisons were made between the following documents: *Hu-shui t'iao-ch'a ch'ing-ts'e* (Household tax investigation record), *T'u-ti fu-chi ts'e* (Land tax record), *Fang-ling nung-hu ch'ing-ts'e shih-shih keng-che yu ch'i t'ien ch'eng-ling nung-hu ch'ing-ts'e* (Register of farm households acquiring land through public sale or through implementation of the Land-to-the-Tiller Act), *Szu-yu keng-ti tsu-yüeh teng-chi p'u* (Records of private cultivating leases), and *Ti-szu chieh keng-ti tsu-t'ien wei-yüan hsüan-chu an-chüan* (Records of the fourth session Landlord-Tenant Arbitration Committee elections).

TABLE 3

Size of Cultivated Holdings in Tatieh, 1952–64

Size of holding (hectares)	1952		1960		1964	
	Number	Percent	Number	Percent	Number	Percent
Under .5	50	24.5%	68	30.4%	80	36.2%
.5–1	57	27.9	69	30.8	64	29.0
1–2	70	34.3	59	26.3	54	24.4
2–3	22	10.8	23	10.3	18	8.1
3–4	3	1.5	2	.9	3	1.4
4–5	2	1.0	3	1.3	2	.9
All households	204	100%	224	100%	221	100%

farm holdings by some 80 hectares, which boosted farm income and investment potential but had little effect on the size of holdings. The progressive reduction in holding size results from population growth.[7] Not only are farm holdings becoming smaller, but variations in their size are also narrowing (see Table 3).

Table 4 suggests that differences in landed wealth in Tatieh are relatively insignificant. Although I cannot, from my records, determine land ownership on a household-by-household basis for

[7] The median holding size declined from .93 hectares in 1952 to .77 hectares in 1964.

TABLE 4
Area Owned by Landowning Households in Tatieh, 1952 and 1964

Area owned (hectares)	1952	1964
Under .5	59	62
.5–1	22	35
1–2	34	32
2–3	15	11
3–4	2	4
4–5	1	2
5–6	5	1
All households	138	147

periods prior to 1953, tax records and interviews all suggest that even in the 1930's the disparity between rich and poor was not much greater than it was in 1952. We might also note that the households owning three or more hectares of land in 1952 and 1964 represented a variety of surnames; no single group in the village had a monopoly on landed wealth.

CHUNGSHE

Chungshe is one of eleven villages in Liuchia township, Tainan county (see Maps 2 and 3). It lies about 30 kilometers northeast of Tainan city. From the village one sees, rising to the east, the same continuous wall of mountains that stood in the background of Tatieh. But Chungshe lies about 50 kilometers to the north of Tatieh, on the Chianan plain. It is nearly as close to the mountains as Tatieh but is 23 kilometers farther from the sea. Chungshe enjoys transportation and communication facilities comparable to those in Tatieh.

As of my 1968 survey, the village contained a total resident population of 1,115, distributed among 194 households. The median household size was 6.0 individuals—exactly the same as in Tatieh. The economically least productive age categories (i.e. under sixteen and over 60) made up 53 percent of the total population. Family structure resembled that in Tatieh. Only 1.6 percent of all households contained families of the "joint" type. The Chianan plain lacks the ethnic diversity characteristic of the Pingtung

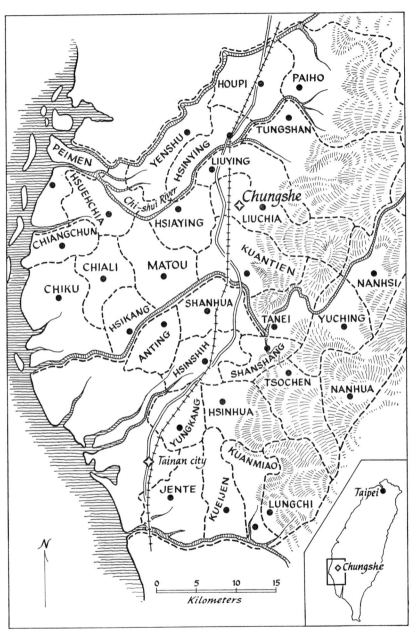

Map 2. Townships of Tainan county

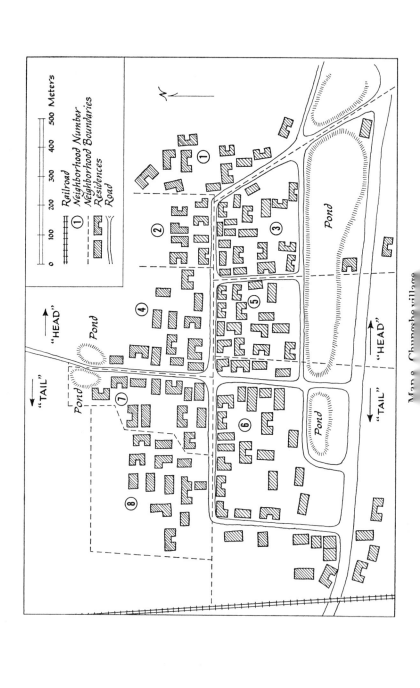

Map 2. Chungshe village

plain. Hokkien speakers have long dominated the entire plain and constitute close to 100 percent of the population in Liuchia township and Chungshe village.

Chungshe means "middle hamlet." On the basis of local legend and a study of genealogical materials, the village appears to have been first settled about 200 years ago by Lai Yüan, who left his brothers in a village near the coast and came here with his sons. Some claim that this ancestor's native village was also called Chungshe and the name was simply carried over. On the other hand, since *she* is often used to designate an aboriginal "hamlet," the village may once have been the dwelling place of aboriginal peoples (Chen Cheng-siang 1963: 37). The history of settlement in this immediate area is not well documented. According to oral traditions, however, it seems that military forces established in the region before the coming of Lai Yüan had already cleared the area of potentially hostile aboriginal people. Older informants consistently told me that Lai Yüan and his sons were the sole inhabitants of what was then an uncultivated frontier area. Lai Yüan certainly managed to obtain control of most of the land in Chungshe. His progeny were joined by other families who came to farm as tenants. According to some of Chungshe's elders, a number of closely related families bearing the surname Ch'en arrived about 50 years after Lai Yüan. They came from a neighboring township to the north and settled in the area of the present village center. Hsü arrived shortly thereafter and also settled near the center of the village. Hsü was followed by Wang and Lin. Families bearing a variety of additional surnames came to the community around 1900 and settled in its western half, colloquially referred to as the village "tail." The eastern portion is called the village "head."

In layout, Chungshe resembles Tatieh. It is compact and nucleated and centers on a crossroads, and its east and west entrances are marked by shrines. Chungshe originally had no community temple; gods were kept in private homes. The first communal structure was built in 1900. The present temple is a simple, square structure, much less lavish than the one in Tatieh and housing

fewer deities. Chungshe's temple doubles as a meeting hall and religious center. Except for special occasions it is closed and lifeless.

By comparison with Tatieh, Chungshe appears impoverished.
The main roads are unpaved and littered. Shabby dwellings of
sun-dried brick and bamboo abound, especially in the village
"tail," many of them with floors of plain packed earth. To a
native of Tatieh, Chungshe might well convey a sense of aban-
donment. Yet there is evidence that a few families in Chungshe
may have achieved a measure of prosperity quite early. For example, there are a number of elaborate kiln-baked brick dwellings
of considerable age in Chungshe, whereas the cement-faced structures so commonplace in Tatieh are actually of recent origin. Electricity was brought to Chungshe as early as 1927, and every home
benefits from it at least minimally.

There are currently twenty surnames represented in Chungshe.
The Lai households constitute 28 percent of all village households.
Forty-five households (83 percent of all the Lai households and 23
percent of all village households) constitute the descendants of
Lai Yüan. The three next most common surnames in the village
are Hsü, Wang, and Lin. These account for 16, 11, and 11 percent
of all village households, respectively. The largest number of Hsü
households that can trace descent from a common ancestor is 24
(77 percent of all Hsü households and 12 percent of all village
households). Thirteen Lin households similarly trace descent from
a common ancestor (62 percent of all Lin households and 7 percent
of all village households). None of the remaining village surnames
account for more than 6 percent of all village households.

The plan and allocation of rooms within the typical compound
in Chungshe are more or less the same as in Tatieh. But in Chungshe, unlike Tatieh, the establishment of a new ancestral hall complete with ancestral tablets is not normally associated with ritual
separation from the parent hall. On numerous ceremonial occasions the inhabitants of a new compound carry sacrifices to more
remote ancestors whose tablets are maintained in other compound
halls. Such ritual bonds between the inhabitants of different compounds in Chungshe reflect the greater solidarity and importance

of the agnatic group in that community. To a greater extent than in Tatieh, furthermore, agnatic groups tend to concentrate in particular portions of the village, so that one's neighbors are commonly also one's agnates.

The vast majority of households in Chungshe were engaged in field cultivation at the time of my fieldwork (1968–69). Although livelihood in both Tatieh and Chungshe depends upon farming, agricultural potentialities in the latter community are somewhat more restricted, especially in terms of climate and soil conditions. Chungshe is located in what is referred to as the "middle and southern normal temperature and normal rainfall district" of Taiwan (*Soils* 1961: 60). The average annual mean temperature for the district as a whole is 73.6°F. The average mean temperature may drop below 68° during the period from December through March. The average annual mean rainfall in the district is 75.9 inches, which is less than in the area of Tatieh village. The season of heaviest rain is also from May through September.

Chungshe's soils are mainly intrazonal, hydromorphic, and planosol-like. They are modified old alluvial soils, characterized by a more or less impervious clay pan and a thin, light-textured surface layer. The yield of crops on these soils is below average, mainly because the compact clay subsoil impedes aeration and effective drainage. Without irrigation they can successfully produce no more than a single crop of rice each year. Even green manure crops cannot be grown in the winter half of the year, and this renders such soils low in organic matter, further increasing the heaviness of their texture. Lands made up of such soils are often referred to as *k'an-t'ien t'ien*, or "fields that depend on the heavens."

About seven kilometers to the west of Chungshe, soils become intrazonal, halomorphic, and saline. They have been sufficiently washed over the years, however, that they lend themselves to the cultivation of rice, sweet potatoes, sugarcane, and peanuts. But crops grown on such soils are dependent on surface moisture only, and this limits total productivity. Growing one crop of rice successfully, or increasing the number of crops grown, requires sup-

TABLE 5

Main Crops Grown in Chungshe Village in 1960

(*hectares*)

Crop	Grand total	Paddy				Upland			
		Sub-total	Winter crop	First crop	Second crop	Sub-total	Winter crop	First crop	Second crop
Paddy rice	191.21	191.21	—	.24	190.97	—	—	—	—
Upland rice	7.52	7.33	—	7.33	—	.19	—	—	.19
Sweet potatoes	105.33	98.80	59.23	39.09	.48	6.53	3.41	.64	2.48
Other beans	12.38	10.83	.01	10.82	—	1.55	—	1.55	—
Sugarcane	36.42	32.90	—	—	—	3.52	—	—	—
Green manure	39.46	38.48	8.19	30.29	—	.98	—	.98	—

SOURCE: Agricultural Census of 1960, data for Chungshe village.

plementing rainfall water with irrigation. Unfortunately, the irrigation potentialities of this region are still very limited (see Chen Cheng-siang 1963: 135–39). As a result, there tends to be competition between farmers in the immediate area of Chungshe, as well as between them and farmers farther to the west, for whatever irrigation water is available.

When properly irrigated and drained, the soils of Chungshe now yield one fall crop of rice and a crop of sweet potatoes each year (see Table 5). Only a small portion of village farmland is capable of producing a spring crop of rice. A few families also own small ponds from which they harvest fish once or twice a year.

As in Tatieh, holding sizes in Chungshe did not differ radically from household to household either on the eve of the Land-to-the-Tiller Program in 1953 or at the time of my field study in 1968. Since 1949, when the Land Reform Program was initiated, the proportion of tenanted land has significantly decreased (see Table 6). All told, about 76 hectares of cultivated land became cultivator-owned during various stages of the Land Reform Program. As in Tatieh, increasing pressure of population has led to a progressive reduction in holding size, and variations in holding size are similarly narrowing (see Table 7). The median cultivated holding in Chungshe decreased from 1.72 hectares in 1949 to 1.07 hectares in 1968 (compare with Tatieh's .93 hectares in 1952 and .77 hectares

TABLE 6

Ownership of Land Cultivated by Chungshe Villagers, 1953–68

Year	Cultivator-owned		Tenant-cultivated	
	Hectares	Percent	Hectares	Percent
1953	103	51%	99	49%
1960	179	81	43	19
1968	206	83	43	17

SOURCE: Figures for 1953 were reconstructed on the basis of data from the following documents: *T'u-ti so-yu-ch'üan jen kuei-hu k'a-p'ien* (Landowner cards), *Szu-yu keng-ti fang-ling ch'ing ts'e* (Records of lands received during implementation of the Land-to-the-Tiller Act), and *Fang-ling kung-yu keng-ti nung-hu ch'ing-ts'e* (Record of lands received during sales of public land). The Committee on Agricultural Census of the Taiwan Provincial Government provided the figures for 1960. Those for 1968 were calculated by me, on the basis of interviews and a comparison of the following documents: *Ts'un t'u-ti ts'e-liao kuei-hu ts'e* (Village landownership record), *Keng-ti tsu-yüeh teng-chi pu* (Record of private cultivating leases), *Szu-yu keng-ti tsu-yüeh fu-pen* (Supplement to the record of private cultivating leases), *Fang-ling keng-ti tsu cheng-shou* (obliterated) *ch'ing-ts'e* (Record of public land rented), and *Ch'i-shui t'iao-ch'a pu* (Records of contract tax investigation).

TABLE 7

Size of Cultivated Holdings in Chungshe, 1953–68

Size of holding (hectares)	1953		1960		1968	
	Number	Percent	Number	Percent	Number	Percent
Under .5	4	4.0%	15	9.7%	30	17.0%
.5–1	14	13.9	35	22.7	52	29.5
1–2	42	41.6	71	46.1	56	31.9
2–3	25	24.8	20	13.0	21	11.9
3–4	8	7.9	9	5.8	12	6.8
4–5	7	6.9	4	2.6	3	1.7
Over 5[a]	1	1.0	—	—	2	1.2
All households	101	100%	154	100%	176	100%

[a] The 1953 holding was between five and six hectares; one of the 1968 holdings was between six and seven hectares, the other between nine and ten.

in 1964). More farmers in Chungshe cultivated holdings of three or more hectares, and a great many more cultivated holdings of one to three hectares.

In terms of landownership, however, we find wide disparities in wealth between individual households as well as between the various surname groups in Chungshe. We are fortunate in having figures on landownership for three points in time for this community (see Table 8). It is significant that all households owning three or more hectares of cultivated land in 1925 were members of one de-

TABLE 8
Area Owned by Landowning Households in Chungshe, 1925–68

Area owned (hectares)	1925[a]	1953	1968
Under .5	22	23	7
.5–1	6	21	14
1–2	9	26	16
2–3	1	7	9
3–4	2	7	5
4–5	1	1	3
5–6	—	1	1
6–7	2	2	2
7–10	1	2	2
10–13	3	1	1
Over 13[b]	3	1	—
All households	50	92	60

[a] Source for 1925: *Tseng-wen chün liu-chia chuang chung-she t'u-ti teng-chi pu* (Land register for Chungshe village).
[b] All four holdings in this row were over twenty hectares.

scent group—the Lai Yüan group, which has dominated the community since its initial settlement. In 1953, twelve out of fifteen households owning three or more hectares belonged to this descent group, and in 1968 ten out of fourteen still did. Although the disparity decreased by 1968, Chungshe continued to be a community in which there were marked differences in terms of landed wealth. It is interesting to note that no households in Tatieh in 1952 or 1964 owned over six hectares of land. In Chungshe there were nine such families in 1925, six in 1953, and five in 1968.

In terms of the descriptions presented thus far, Tatieh and Chungshe do not appear dramatically different. As we shall see, however, there are contrasts between the two communities that, while not immediately obvious, are nonetheless significant. In the following chapters we shall examine these differences and suggest some of the factors that have played a major role in generating them. Ultimately, in conjunction with other materials from southeastern China, our comparison of Tatieh and Chungshe suggests two hypotheses. One is that small agnatic groups were most likely to develop into single-lineage communities on open frontiers where competition for strategic resources was minimal, whereas the need for cooperation across agnatic lines for purposes of exploiting the environment or for defense tended to generate or reinforce the development of multi-lineage communities. Another is that higher-order (i.e. nonlocalized) descent groups resulting from an aggregative process seem to be associated with situations where territorially discrete and numerically weak agnatic groups have been confronted by a large and persistent common enemy.

TWO

Agriculture

WHERE SUBSISTENCE is largely based on farming, interactions mediating access to agricultural resources and articulations involved in their use and maintenance assume special importance. In both Tatieh and Chungshe subsistence is mainly derived from paddy rice. Land, water, labor, and capital constitute major resources without which this particular form of cultivation would not be possible. In comparing the importance of various forms of affiliation in these villages, therefore, it is essential that we determine the kinds of relations involved in the manipulation of these resources.

The main difference between Tatieh and Chungshe concerning access to subsistence resources is that cooperation across agnatic lines was less essential in Chungshe. Whereas access to land and capital in Tatieh has in no significant way been linked to agnatic affiliation, agricultural labor and the management of water resources have involved extensive cooperation across agnatic lines. In Chungshe, on the other hand, a single descent group long managed to maintain a grip over the village economy by controlling access to land and capital, and agnatic affiliation played a more important role in the organization of labor. Most important, irrigation in Chungshe did not require or encourage cooperation until 1930.

TATIEH

According to landlord-tenant contracts registered in compliance with the rent Reduction Act of 1949, about 70 percent of all the households registered in Tatieh were tenanting at least some of the land they cultivated. Only 18.4 percent were in the landlord category. The remaining 11.2 percent must have been either full owners with no land rented out or noncultivating households.[1] In view of the high rate of tenancy just prior to the land reforms, we might begin by discussing the nature of the landlord-tenant relationship. We should also determine the identity of the landlords and the extent to which various forms of affiliation were crucial to the landlord-tenant relationship.

Land. Before implementation of the Rent Reduction Program, the so-called *t'ieh-tsu,* or "iron rent," system prevailed in Tatieh as it did in most of Taiwan. Rents were paid in kind, the amount being stipulated in advance on the basis of normal yield expectancy. Just prior to 1949, rent on an average hectare of paddy in this area amounted to about 48 percent of annual main-crop yield.[2] In the event of natural calamity a tenant could appeal to his landlord for a rent reduction, but success or failure in this respect depended entirely on the particular nature of their relationship.

According to local custom, rent could not be raised without notice of at least one season and a tenant could not be arbitrarily denied the harvest on land he had planted. Landlord-tenant agreements were oral. They were rarely violated, however, and were customarily renewed unless a landlord needed the land himself or if the tenant failed to pay his rent for some time. Tenants were not expected to provide voluntary service, gifts, or securities. Where a relationship could use deepening, however, a tenant might find it "advisable" to send his landlord a pair of chickens at New Year's time. Payment of the land tax and irrigation fees was the landlord's responsibility.

The landlord-tenant relationship in Tatieh was less harsh than that reported for the island generally (cf. Chang Yen-tien 1954:

---

[1] Statements on tenancy in 1949 are based on data in the *T'ien-nung k'a-p'ien* (Tenant cards) and the *Ti-chu k'a-p'ien* (Landlord cards). The total number of households registered in 1949 was obtained from the *Hu-chi t'ung-chi yüeh pao-piao* (Household register monthly statistical reports).

[2] Rents on cultivated land belonging to lineages and corporate associations were somewhat lower, amounting to about 33 percent of annual yield.

6–13; and Chen Cheng 1961: 8–10). Nevertheless, a tenant's security and subsistence ultimately depended upon the impression his landlord had of him, mediated to some extent by sanctions of custom and public opinion. The landlord was not only a source of land but an important source of credit and capital in a situation where subsistence depended upon the availability of capital. If a landlord was favorably disposed toward his tenant, the latter might approach him for a loan or ask him to participate in a grain association (or credit club).

Who were these landlords upon whom so many villagers depended? In 1949, about 87 percent of the 111 hectares of cultivated land tenanted by Tatieh farmers was located within the village boundaries. The tenancy contracts of 1949 indicate that 54 percent of village tenanted land was owned by 36 Hokkien owners living outside Hsinpi township. No kin relationship could be traced between villagers and their absentee landlords. About 69 percent of all leases were with individual landlords of different surname, and about 75 percent of all contracts involving village landlords were signed with tenants of different surname. It should be noted that identity of surname does not, by itself, indicate a patrilineal relationship. These facts suggest no preference for renting land to agnatic kinsmen. Villagers indicate that renting land to kinsmen of any sort is to be avoided because embarrassment might arise should landlord and tenant become involved in a dispute. In terms of access to land through tenancy prior to the land reform, then, most villagers had to depend upon persons to whom they were not closely related.

As a result of the Land Reform Program, the relationship between landlord and tenant was legally defined, the total area of tenanted land diminished, and the number of resident and absentee landlords reduced (see Table 9). Absentee landlords in 1964 still consisted mainly of Hokkien owners in Tungkang. Table 10 indicates the distribution of absentee landlords, individual and corporate, according to residence and area rented out to Tatieh villagers in that year.

Conflicts that erupted elsewhere on the island when the Rent

TABLE 9

*Number of Resident and Absentee Landlords and Areas of
Cultivated Land Tenanted by Tatieh Villagers, 1952 and 1964*

Category	1952	1964
Total cultivated area		
tenanted (hectares)	116.04	29.40
Resident landlords		
Number	47	25
Hectares	33.86	15.95
Absentee landlords		
Number	30	14
Hectares	82.18	13.45

Reduction Program was implemented seem to have been relatively mild in Tatieh, but the few villagers that were landlords felt some bitterness. They complain to this day that old "friendships" were summarily obliterated as former tenants grew "cold" and "disrespectful." One reason for the relative lack of conflict in Tatieh was that there were no really big landlords, absentee or resident. Of 48 resident landlords, 31 were renting out under one hectare of land in 1949 and only one as much as fifteen hectares. Out of 36 absentee landlords, twenty were renting less than one hectare and the largest only six or seven hectares. When we consider that there were landlords in Tungkang renting out more than 100 hectares of land, the amount rented in Tatieh seems insignificant.

Investment in land for the purpose of renting it to tenants is no longer good business. When the Rent Reduction Program was initiated, the annual rent on one hectare of average paddy in the Pingtung area amounted to about 2,625 catties of rice. This constituted 37.5 percent of a standard annual main-crop yield of 7,000 catties.[3] Although productivity rose to about 16,000 catties per annum by 1964, rent remained the same. In 1964, then, the landlord was receiving only 16.4 percent of actual yield. While he receives a progressively smaller proportion of yield, his expenses have increased. Land taxes have risen, and, although the landlord is now required to pay only half of the irrigation fees, by 1964

[3] See Chang Yen-tien (1954: 29) for a table of grade-yield equivalences. One catty equals .59682 kilogram.

TABLE 10
Absentee Landlords, by Residence and Area Rented to
Tatieh Villagers in 1964

Category	Number	Hectares
All absentee landlords	14	13.45
Tungkang residents	6	7.27
Chiatung residents	4	3.27
Sugar refinery	1	2.56
Other	3	.35

these had risen to about six times what they had been in 1949. The landlord's annual tax and irrigation costs on an average hectare of paddy in 1964 added up to about 1,028 catties (with all fees converted into rice), while his rent amounted to only 2,635 catties. Profit per year was thus 1,597 catties, which in 1964 was worth NT$3,753.[4] If the landlord could have sold this land untenanted in 1964, he could have realized an estimated NT$200,000 on the transaction; invested in a bank this sum would earn NT$2,500 each month. If he grew bananas on this hectare, he might have earned between NT$50,000 and NT$100,000 during the year, even if all labor had been hired. Growing rice with hired labor would probably have brought him about NT$25,000.[5]

That tenancy continues to exist at all is due to the fact that the Rent Reduction Act made it virtually impossible for a landlord to reclaim tenanted land. Article 19 of the Act states that a landlord may not repossess cultivated land upon expiration of a lease (1) if he is unable to cultivate it himself, (2) if his total income is sufficient to support his family, or (3) if loss of this land would deprive the tenant's family of its subsistence. Up until the end of 1964, there had been no cases in Tatieh of landlords successfully reclaiming land on these grounds.[6] The only realistic way for a landlord

[4] At the official rate of exchange in 1964, NT$1.00 was worth US$.40.

[5] The NT$200,000 estimate is based on prices actually paid and received in Tatieh during 1964; the other figures are based on informant estimates.

[6] I base this statement on a study of cases that appeared before the Township Landlord-Tenant Arbitration Committee from 1952 through 1964. A record of such cases is to be found in the Tsu-t'ien wei-yüan hui chuan-tsung (Records of the Landlord-Tenant Committee).

to reclaim tenanted land is to appeal to his tenant through mutual friends and to offer a compensation equivalent to half the current property value. This procedure has worked in a number of cases. The selling price of tenanted land is low because existing leases are not automatically terminated. The price of untenanted land, on the other hand, has been rising year after year.[7] If a landlord's need for land exceeds the size of his cultivated holding, therefore, it is cheaper for him to retrieve tenanted land than to buy untenanted land.

Apart from tenancy and purchase directly related to the land Reform Program there is another avenue for the acquisition of land. Cultivated land may be sold or given away. Villagers say that land to be sold ought to be offered to close agnates first. Actually, it is considered "embarrassing" to do so. Relatives in need of land are not always able to pay the best price; and should a relative attempt to bargain, the seller would find himself in an unpleasant position. Preferential rights of agnates notwithstanding, the data indicate that voluntary sales or gifts of land do not normally involve closely related persons. From 1952 through 1963, a total of 255 voluntary land transactions were registered by Tatieh villagers. Only 17 percent involved former tenants. Agnates were the recipients in only 15 percent of the cases. The bulk of transfers, about 85 percent, were made to persons with whom there was no close relationship. It is clear, then, that access to land through purchase or tenancy does not depend upon kinship.

Although the Land Reform Program did level differences of wealth in Tatieh, it apparently did not produce the "leadership vacuum" or "social disorganization" that Gallin describes (1963: 110–12). There were not fewer leaders in the village after the land reform but rather leaders of greater variety. Sources of influence have broadened. Wealth and landownership no longer constitute the only sources of power and influence; range of contacts, technical sophistication, bureaucratic position, and level of education

[7] According to informants, an average hectare of grade ten paddy sold for about NT$2,000 in 1940. By 1965, purchase of the same piece of land required an investment of NT$2–300,000.

have become increasingly important. There has not been a displacement of former leaders in Tatieh as much as a diffusion of power and influence.

Irrigation. Henry Orenstein recently proposed that "where all or most land in a community is canal-irrigated, it is possible that conflict will become intense and widespread, and the farmer, instead of cooperating with his neighbor, may become isolated from him" (1965: 1531). Orenstein further suggested that in certain cases militarism and the subjection of one community by another may be generated not so much by population pressure as by inequalities in access to irrigation water. These observations are supported by other researchers. According to Hsiao Kung-chuan, disputes over water constituted the most important and most frequent causes of feuding in traditional China (1960: 419). And R. H. Tawney wrote (1966: 46):

> The cooperation—and quarreling—which, in the European village, had their occasion in the maintenance of the common course of cultivation, and the regulation of the use of common pastures, meadows and woods, by the court of the manor, in China finds its most striking expression in the control of water; in some regions, for example, if a canal runs through a number of villages, each village uses it in turn by agreement, the time of use by each farmer being regulated by the burning of an incense stick, and the disputes being appropriately settled in the temple of the God of War.

The implication of Tawney's remarks is that the same factors that underlie conflict and feuding may also generate cooperative networks and structures to preclude or alleviate the expression of hostility. It stands to reason that the nature of such structures will depend upon the requirements of the irrigation systems involved.

Water is the second ingredient vital to paddy rice agriculture as it is practiced in Tatieh. The problem is to regulate the supply of water in such a way as to eliminate flooding during the rainy season and ensure an adequate, equitable supply during the dry season. The 220 hectares of privately owned farmland in Tatieh are watered by six main canal systems. The P'u-wei network is the most important, furnishing water to over 100 hectares in Tatieh alone, and also to fields in neighboring communities. The main canal was originally supplied entirely by underground flow originating in the Lin-pien River. Since 1956, six high-voltage pumping stations have been built at various points along the main canal to counterbalance the drying up of older sources and to ensure more equitable and timely distribution. A number of privately owned gas or diesel-driven pipe wells scattered throughout the area provide temporary boosts to the water supply when necessary.

When a group of farmers desires to have a permanent pumping station constructed to service a given area, it applies to the irrigation association for "water rights" to that area.[8] Once such rights have been granted, no other pumps may legally be built within the designated area. The irrigation association obtains a loan from the Land Bank on behalf of the farmers to cover the costs of constructing the pump. The farmers to be serviced by this pump collectively guarantee to repay the loan and the interest. The portion of payment allocated to each farmer depends upon the area serviced in each case.

One needs to have some notion of how Tatieh's irrigation system works to appreciate the degree to which cooperation is required and the form it will take. The way any particular field obtains water depends upon its distance from the nearest source and its height relative to that source. If a field is higher than the nearest source, water must be led to it from a more distant one. Most fields do not obtain water directly from canals but from higher fields. Several methods may be used to convey water from one field to another depending upon the relative sizes of the fields, the nature of their soils, etc. Regardless of the method selected, however, a number of field openings and closures are required and a considerable amount of supervision is necessary. Some form of cooperation between field owners must be established.

Irrigation and drainage systems are equipped with a variety of

[8] Irrigation associations are self-administered organizations that operate with government approval and support. Civil powers vested in them enable them to levy workers, acquire land, and collect fees from farmers within their jurisdiction. They are administratively responsible for the maintenance of local irrigation systems and for the arbitration of irrigation disputes.

dams and locks to store water and direct its flow. Manipulation of these facilities enables equitable distribution of water on a rotational basis during the dry season and drainage during the wet season. Most households own from two to four fields located in different places. Since each must be filled, drained, and regulated at various points in the growing season, any given farmer will find himself coordinating his activities with a number of other farmers. He must cooperate not only with the owners of adjacent fields but also with farmers farther up and down the canal. When it comes to cooperation in irrigation, the most important factor is not kinship but relative location of fields with respect to water source. If one were to plot the distribution of fields in terms of surname, the interposition of surnames would become strikingly clear. Not only are there few concentrated areas associated with particular surnames, but even where small blocs do appear they are found on a line with fields belonging to other surnames.

Each main canal system constitutes a *hsiao-tsu*, or "small group." The small group chief, elected once every three years, is responsible for collecting irrigation fees, disseminating information passed down from the irrigation association, and assisting in the arbitration of disputes arising within the group. Each branch of the main canal constitutes a subgroup under an elected subgroup chief. The fourteen subgroups in the P'u-wei system hold no regular meetings and are units only for purposes of cleaning tributary canals. Of particular importance are unofficial groups formed on the basis of immediate water source. It is within and between these groups that rotation and coordination mainly occur. Since a farmer usually owns fields in several locations, he normally belongs to several such groups. Within each, a good many people will not be related to him.

To every permanent pumping station the irrigation association assigns a watchman, usually on the basis of recommendations provided by pump group members. He is responsible for day and night security of this pump. His salary is paid directly by the irrigation association, which then collects the wage from the farmers serviced. During the dry season a pump group will also employ one or two field watchmen. Their wages are paid directly by the field owners. Once a rotation schedule has been agreed upon, it is the field watchman's job to implement it. He can make no changes without prior authorization from all group members. At the same time, however, his employment constitutes a relinquishment of individual rights to control water flow. It becomes the field watchman's duty to patrol the fields day and night, to regulate and direct flow, and to prevent unauthorized diversion of water. Kinship plays no role in the selection of pump and field watchmen. They are usually enlisted from outside the group on the basis of their reputation for responsibility, good judgment, and fairness. Only poorer villagers are normally interested in becoming pump or field watchmen, especially the latter, who must bear the brunt of group tensions during periods of drought.

Figure 1 illustrates the operation of rotational irrigation as well as the nature of coordination within and between groups. In 1963, area C received water from pumps 1 and 2 for one day each week during the period of rotation. On these days water was allowed to bypass areas A and B. Pump station 4 was not yet operative and station 3 was not equipped to draw sufficient water to supply both area C and area D. When areas A and B were watered, a rotation schedule was also set up between them such that one received water at night while the other was irrigated by day. One year later, the construction of station 4 was completed. In addition, a second pipe was installed at station 3 and a diesel-driven pipe well (5) was set up in area B. As a result of these improvements, the water supply was augmented and the pattern of rotation modified. All four areas are now independent; rotation largely takes place within rather than between them.

Prior to the introduction of spaced pumping stations, cooperative networks were larger and included more farmers. Because access to water was less reliable and less predictable, conflicts were common and often severe. As far back as memory or record can take us, cooperation appears to have been essential to irrigation in the region. In an unpublished manuscript entitled "Researches

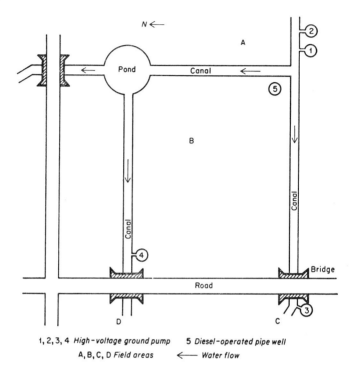

1, 2, 3, 4 *High-voltage ground pump*   5 *Diesel-operated pipe well*
A, B, C, D *Field areas*   ←— *Water flow*

Fig. 1. Rotational irrigation on a section of the
P'u-wei canal system in Tatieh

on the Migrations of Hakka in Kaohsiung and Pingtung Counties," Liu Chao-shu described early irrigation activities on the
Pingtung plain (see also Chung Jen-shou n.d., and *Wan-luan*
1971).[9] According to Liu, when the Hakka first arrived in the area
they dammed rivers and valleys to form reservoirs from which
canals were used to direct water flow. Wells were built to tap underground sources. Joint efforts were required to construct, maintain, and defend irrigation facilities; large projects involved several villages, smaller ones scores of households.

Around 1916, the sugar refinery in nearby Nanchou began to

[9] Liu Chao-shu is a pseudonym for an author whose name I am not at liberty
to reveal. Although the manuscript is undated, Liu informs me that it was
largely completed after 1945.

bring virgin dryland under sugar cultivation. The area of sugarcane was extended into Tatieh in the 1930's. To ensure proper
flood control and irrigation for the refinery's expanding acreage,
a number of water control projects were constructed that altered
the nature of irrigation throughout the area. Between 1916 and
1918, three retaining dams were built where mountain streams
meet the plain to form the Lin-pien River. Underground flow was
stored in the valley for use during the dry winter months. The
effect of these dams on private farmers in the area was immediate
and profound. During the dry season springs and wells dried up.
Underground flow could not take place so long as the upper
reaches of the Lin-pien were nearly dry. When flooding occurred,
on the other hand, the refinery protected its fields by dumping
water into the riverbed. As a result, farmers in the township suffered from augmented flooding. Between 1933 and 1936 a series of
dikes was constructed along the banks of the Lin-pien to reduce
flooding. At the same time, however, these dikes further reduced
the winter water table and accentuated drought. As a result, farmers found themselves struggling over water. Farmers farther from
the source had to wait longer to prepare their fields. This problem
was considerably alleviated with the introduction of pumping stations, but conflict over water is still quite common. During periods
of drought, the frequency of irrigation group meetings increases
drastically. Anxiety and hostility permeate the community, and
farmers stay up at night to patrol their fields and double-check
the watchmen.

When meetings are called to solve problems and resolve disputes, farmers align themselves in terms of field position rather
than kinship. Under some circumstances even brothers oppose
each other. When normal water supplies become inadequate, irrigation groups frequently find it necessary to rent additional
pumps. Kinship plays little role in determining the choice of
pump owner or the price to be paid.

Labor. Labor constitutes the third resource essential to agriculture. Household labor in Tatieh is normally sufficient to meet a
family's day-to-day requirements—to raise three or four pigs and

some poultry, and to carry out routine care of fields and crops. But the agricultural cycle is characterized by peaks of intense labor demand alternating with periods of relative surplus. At times of maximal demand, household labor becomes inadequate and other sources must be exploited.

Where water resources are limited in terms of quantity or time of access, the possibility exists for cooperation in the form of labor exchange between households. While some farmers are drawing water from the irrigation system for field preparation, others wait their turn. Exchanges may be made between village households or between families in different communities. Where household labor is not available for exchange, labor may be hired. Finally, an arrangement known as "help" may be preferred. In this case labor is obtained from another household without expectation of an immediate return in kind or wage. Households receiving "help" are obliged to return "help" when called upon, in any form that may be needed.

Whether labor is hired or exchanged, the work involved in harvesting and transplanting is almost always accomplished by team effort. There are ten transplanting and eight harvesting groups in Tatieh. Transplanting teams range in size from six to fifteen members, and the major criteria for membership are ability to perform the tasks involved and a cooperative disposition. Harvesting teams are structurally similar, but skill is less a requisite of participation. Neither kinship nor neighborhood plays a special role in determining team composition. The workers are friends who feel that they can get along and work well together. Work done is remunerated either in kind (exchange labor) or in wages.

Employers choose teams mainly on the basis of their reliability and availability. Even if a farmer has a household member working with a particular team for the purpose of obtaining labor on an exchange basis, that team's services may be unavailable when he needs them. If he is concerned that the rain might come before his crop has been harvested, for example, he may decide to forfeit his turn on the team schedule and find a group available earlier. The wage earnings of his family member will be applied to the cost of hiring another team.

The recent introduction of permanent water-pumping stations has significantly altered the relationship between labor supply and demand. Water has suddenly become available to most villagers at about the same time. More farmers are in a position to prepare, transplant, and harvest their fields within a shorter period, and labor demand has become at once more brief and more intense. With everyone busy at about the same time, fewer farmers are able to release labor for exchange and team labor is becoming increasingly difficult to obtain locally.

Farmers try to plant their rice as early as possible in order to take advantage of the higher rice prices that are possible with an early harvest. More important, when the first rice crop is planted early there is a better chance of harvesting it before the summer rains begin. Wet grain is more difficult to harvest, winnow, and dry. Worse yet, kernels that get wet and sprout on the stem are unsalable. The second crop should be planted as early as possible to ensure sufficient time after harvest to plant and fully mature a winter soybean crop.

Soybeans became a widespread winter crop in this area in 1964. As a consequence, labor demand during the harvest of the second rice crop has become greater than at any other time in the agricultural cycle. Soybeans have a long maturation period; if they are not planted immediately after the second rice harvest, it could become necessary to plow them under. Labor that would otherwise be liberated after the rice harvest is immediately tied down again.

Since unit area yields are higher now than ever before, farmers can no longer wait until all fields have been harvested before they begin to process their rice. Winnowing and drying now take place as the rice is being brought in, and this ties more household labor down. Yet another factor has contributed to the shortening and intensification of periods of labor demand. Power tillers, introduced in the area around 1960, have increased in number. It costs no more to prepare a field using a power tiller and a buffalo than using a buffalo alone, and takes much less time.[10] Tillers have the

---

[10] Field preparation includes plowing, harrowing, and flattening. Power tillers are used to accomplish only the first step; harrowing and flattening are still done with the buffalo.

further advantage of being able to operate at night. More than half of all village farmers now hire tiller owners to prepare their fields. In 1964 Tatieh villagers owned twelve such machines, and at harvest additional tillers were brought into the village from as far away as Meinung. Where tiller units are hired, there is rarely a kinship connection between the operator and his employer. The most important factor is availability.

Pumps and power tillers have had a similar effect throughout the surrounding area. Timing differences between villages and townships have been dramatically reduced, and labor must increasingly be brought in from more distant places. Employer-employee relationships now cut across not only kinship and regional lines, but ethnic lines as well. Though villagers prefer not to hire outside labor, alternatives are increasingly difficult to find. Farmers frequently complain that outsiders, particularly non-Hakka, are inefficient and unreliable. On one occasion, a villager promised a Hokkien group that if they would come to work for him he would arrange other jobs for them in the community. In keeping with this pledge he scheduled them to harvest the fields of five or six other families. After the workers completed some of their work, they were tempted to leave Tatieh to accept employment for higher wages elsewhere. By this time it would have been too late for the farmers depending on them to find other labor. Their village host found it necessary to hold them in the community by threatening not to help them collect their wages from the farmers whose fields had already been completed.

The labor supply-demand formula has been significantly altered in recent years, but there are also continuities. In the acquisition and organization of labor for agriculture, value continues to be placed on maximizing community self-sufficiency. Villagers—be they friends, agnates, affines, or whatever—are more to be trusted than outsiders. Beyond the community, Hakka are more reliable than Hokkien.

Capital and credit. In recent years the village has invested more in production and spent more for ceremonies, housing, clothing, food, and other consumer goods. Earnings and living standards have shown marked improvement, but when total expenditures are subtracted from gross income most household budgets just about balance. Farm incomes reflect peaks corresponding to harvest periods. Unusual expenditures must be planned long in advance. An unanticipated emergency, such as a death, can plunge a family deeply into debt.

Capital may be borrowed from a variety of sources, the most important of which is the traditional *ku-hui*, or "grain association." Most farmers belong to at least one such group, so as to be able to borrow relatively large amounts of rice (or money) for long periods at rates of interest comparable to those provided by banks (cf. Fei 1939: 267–74). Principal and interest are paid in semiannual installments over a period of years, and the borrower is not required to provide guarantors, since most group members are fellow villagers and either friends or relatives. Kinship is a peripheral factor in determining membership. The organizer, typically motivated by an immediate need of funds, basically looks among his friends for those with capital to invest. People join for a variety of reasons. For one thing, investment constitutes a form of banking; a member of the group who anticipates that he will need a considerable sum of money at some time in the future knows that he can bid high for the fund when he needs it. More important than the banking or profit-making aspects of participation is the belief that mutual obligation and reciprocity require it.

If a farmer cannot afford to wait until the next harvest, when he can bid for a grain association fund, he must turn to other sources of capital and credit. The government and various cooperative agencies provide loans to farmers, usually for specific productive purposes (e.g. pig raising, banana cultivation, purchase of power tillers). Villagers frequently take advantage of such sources, but they are less popular than grain associations because of the complications involved (e.g. requirement of guarantors, shorter repayment terms). Loans at higher rates of interest may also be obtained from private parties in or out of the community. Private lenders may or may not be kinsmen. Small loans may be made from close agnates for short periods, and no interest is normally charged in such cases; but those who need larger sums for longer periods can rarely depend on relatives.

Many villagers considered it inadvisable to borrow from relatives unless they were co-members of a grain association from which the loan was obtained. Even when a relative has money to spare, a request for a loan would be "embarrassing" for both parties. It is painful to ask for help and even more difficult to ignore an appeal. The borrower cannot be sure whether to offer interest, and the lender whether to accept such an offer. In most cases, then, money is borrowed from nonkinsmen.

CHUNGSHE

Landlord-tenant conditions in Chungshe were not radically different from those in Tatieh prior to the land reforms, but there are indications that they were relatively harsh and formal. Rents were higher and landlords more exploitative. These facts, combined with the apparent insecurity of tenancy, suggest that landlords in Chungshe were not as constrained by public opinion as those in Tatieh.

Land. In 1953, on the eve of the Land-to-the-Tiller Act, 45 percent of all land rented by Chungshe villagers was rented from village landlords; absentee landlords provided 55 percent. (In Tatieh just a few years earlier it was 29 percent resident ownership and 71 percent absentee ownership.) Most of Chungshe's landlords, like their counterparts in Tatieh, were renting out small areas of land: out of 29 resident landlords, fifteen were renting under one hectare. A few, however, were renting out substantial areas of land: five were renting over six hectares, and one was renting out between 26 and 27 hectares.[11] Whereas landlords in Tatieh belonged to a miscellany of agnatic groups, most of Chungshe's village landlords were descendants of Lai Yüan. Of these, 31 percent belonged to the Chieh-kao sublineage and 21 percent were members of the Chieh-kuei sublineage. The economic supremacy of

[11] The sources for figures for early 1953 and 1968 in Chungshe are those indicated in a note to Table 6, p. 17.

the Lai Yüan lineage is even more clearly reflected in the amount of land rented out. Of a total of 95 hectares rented by village landlords, 93 percent belonged to members of this descent group (73 percent to members of the Chieh-kao sublineage and 17 percent to members of the Chieh-kuei sublineage). It is not surprising that the Chieh-kao sublineage is also the most highly segmented one in terms of lineage estates. Lineage segmentation reflects the differential distribution of wealth within this descent group.

As in Tatieh, access to land through tenancy prior to the Land-to-the-Tiller Program was not dependent upon agnatic kinship. Only 23 percent of all farmers renting land from villagers had the same surname as their landlords (as compared with 25 percent in Tatieh). In both communities there was a conscious effort to avoid renting land to close relatives. This fact further highlights the importance of Lai Yüan's descendants as sources of land in Chungshe.

Landlordism sharply declined in Chungshe as a direct result of the Land-to-the-Tiller Program. In early 1953, 28 percent of all cultivating households were renting out some land; in 1968, only 6 percent were renting out land. The area rented out by village landlords decreased from 95 hectares in early 1953 to 25 hectares in 1968. The diminished importance of village landlordism was not accomplished without considerable tension. The Land-to-the-Tiller Program stimulated ill feelings between landlord and tenant that persist to this day. Because virtually all village landlords were members of a single descent group, localized in one part of the village, and because nearly half of all tenanted land was rented from them, antagonisms were phrased in terms of an opposition between the descendants of Lai Yüan and all other villagers. Tenants resent their former domination by the Lai, and the latter generally complain about the ingratitude and jealousy of other villagers. Sometimes this antagonism is expressed not in terms of surname directly, but in terms of village section. People living in the village "head" claim that those in the "tail" are illiterate, lazy, alcoholic, and prone to gambling and violence. On one occasion, when two young men got into argument and a knifing resulted, villagers in the "head" explained that violence of this sort was to be expected from the crude, uneducated inhabitants of the "tail." Villagers in the "tail," for their part, regard those in the "head" as snobbish, arrogant, selfish, and greedy. Cleavages within the community in terms of residence, descent group, and wealth are related and are manifested in many ways, as we shall see when we take up village integration.

Villagers in Chungshe, like those in Tatieh, feel that property to be sold should first be offered to close agnatic kinsmen. I have seen old contracts of sale which specifically state that the land sold had been so offered. It is said that "in former times" the sale of land was taken as an indication of declining fortunes that reflected upon the agnatic group as a whole. If a man was so pressed as to have to sell land, his agnates would usually discuss the matter among themselves and make every effort to find a buyer from within the descent group. Villagers observe with admiration that the powerful Liu lineage in nearby Liuying never sold land to a non-Liu until the war years. And records of voluntary sales and purchases of land in Chungshe from 1961 through 1967 indicate that fully 43 percent of all transactions involving villagers were between individuals of the same surname.[12] (Compare 29 percent in Tatieh from 1953 to 1963.) The difference may well reflect the relatively greater emphasis given to agnatic bonds by people in Chungshe.

Irrigation. Tatieh is located in a region of relatively short and essentially independent canals. Irrigation requires cooperation between households and, to a lesser extent, between farmers in neighboring communities. Chungshe lies within an irrigation system that could not operate effectively on the same basis.

The Chianan plain is the largest in Taiwan (4,884 square kilometers). It shares with the Pingtung plain an annual alternation between dry and wet periods, but it lacks the groundwater resources that would make a comparable use of pumps possible. Before the Japanese arrived, yields per unit area on the plain were

---

[12] My source here is *Ch'i-shui t'iao-ch'a pu* (Records of contract tax investigation).

poor.[13] In Tatieh it had always been possible to grow two crops of rice a year. In Chungshe only one crop of rice could be grown, and even this crop was very unreliable because of a widespread dependence on rainfall. Shortly after the Japanese took Taiwan, they devised a plan to increase the area under canal irrigation from about 5,000 hectares to 150,000 hectares. To do this they built, in the 1920's, the Chianan irrigation system, which is still Taiwan's largest and most integrated irrigation system.

Most of the water supplied to the Chianan system is drawn from two sources, the Tseng-wen and Cho-shui rivers (see Map 4). Water from the Tseng-wen is led to a great reservoir, and from there to a northern and southern main canal. These in turn feed water to lateral canals, which provide water to lesser canals and farm ditches throughout the plain. Even given this elaborate system, there is not sufficient water for all farmers on the plain to grow a crop of rice each year. For this reason a three-year rotation schedule has been established for most of the plain such that on any given piece of land one crop of paddy rice, a crop of sugarcane, and a crop of sweet potatoes may be grown within a three-year period (assuming no supplementary sources of water). Access to water is equalized by a managerial division of the entire rotation area into what are called "small areas," of 150 hectares each. One third of each small area is irrigated for rice. Another third is irrigated for sugarcane. The third portion is in dry crops and receives no water at all. In other words, the three segments of each small area are always in different stages of the three-year, three-crop cycle. This means that throughout the plain only one-third of each small area has to be furnished water for paddy rice.

Putting the rotation plan into effect is a complex matter, as the operation of the Wu-shan-tou portion of the system (serving Chungshe) may illustrate. Water is furnished to the main canal every day from June 1 to October 10. During this period all the water in the canals is intended for the rice-growing areas. In De-

13 See *Report on the 1964 Irrigated Land Survey of Irrigation Associations in Taiwan, The Republic of China* (prepared by the Provincial Water Conservancy Bureau), pp. 326–27.

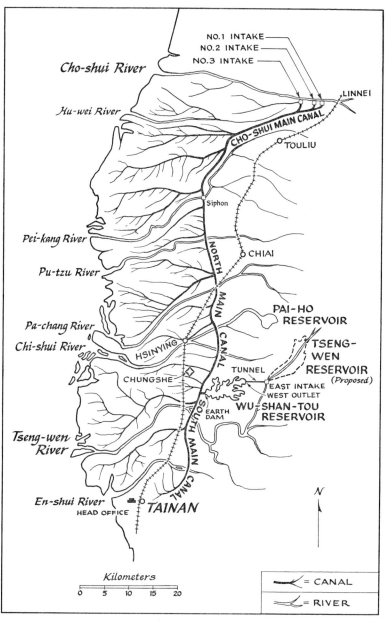

Map 4. The Chianan irrigation system

cember all gates are opened for a period of approximately twelve days for the irrigation of dry crops. For fifteen days in February or March, the canals are again filled to supply water for the cultivation of sugarcane. When newly released irrigation water has reached the two terminal points of the main canal and water levels have been determined to be correct, all exiting gates are simultaneously opened. Two or three times a day while these gates are open, the water level is checked at various points along the canal and adjustments are made to keep it constant. As water is led into each lateral canal, gates exiting from it are partially opened, starting from the top gate and working down, as water passes each gate. When the water has reached the end of the line, the level of water at various points along the lateral canal is checked and adjusted. Thus, all gates in the system are actually kept open at the same time, and their apertures are adjusted as necessary.

Chungshe and a number of neighboring communities draw water from the same lateral canal. In no sense can this particular canal be considered independent of the Chianan irrigation system, since it is drawing water from the same source as all other lateral canals. A loss of water because of theft or mismanagement anywhere on the system can have repercussions everywhere else. An element not found in Tatieh must therefore be added here. Overall operation of the irrigation network depends upon professional coordination (in addition to farmer cooperation)—upon a constant managerial presence. The coordinating agency is the Chianan Irrigation Association. At the local level, however, channeling of water and the resolution of most disputes are still largely handled, as in Tatieh, on a face-to-face basis.

As noted earlier, building, maintaining, and defending irrigation facilities in the area of Tatieh have always required cooperation across agnatic lines. This was especially the case before the introduction of pumps, which led to a contraction of cooperative networks. But before completion of the Chianan system the situation in Chungshe was very different. With rainfall practically the only source of irrigation, there was little need for cooperation of the sort required in Tatieh.

A few canals had been constructed on the Chianan plain before
the arrival of the Japanese. These were mostly small, private enterprises that drew water from nearby rivers to irrigate the land of
the canal owners. In the vicinity of Chungshe, however, there were
no such canals. A small portion of the community's farmland was
watered from public or private ponds scattered about the landscape. Some of these ponds were collectively built by agnatic
groups and subsequently reserved as ancestral properties. In all
such instances the people involved were progeny of Lai Yüan.
Except for the small area of village farmland that drew water
from these ponds, Chungshe's cultivated land was exclusively dependent on rainfall. As we have seen, fields watered in this fashion
were colloquially referred to as *k'an-t'ien t'ien*, or "fields that depend on the heavens." Every household owned at least one buffalo
and began field preparation immediately after the onset of the
rains. Since one could never be sure how long it would rain, or
when it might rain again, it was imperative that the job be accomplished as soon and as quickly as possible. Field ridges were
kept very high so rain could be stored in the field, commonly 30–35
inches rather than the present 12–14 inches. Intermittent irrigation is more desirable from the point of view of yield, but it requires considerably more labor because water has to be moved
about many times and because weed growth is greater. In Chungshe, therefore, water dropped into one's field from the heavens
rather than from adjacent fields and canals. Once in the fields, it
remained there. Cooperation was minimal, and so was water theft.

Under optimal conditions, as I have indicated, most farmers
could grow only one crop of rice each year. With completion of
the Chianan project, farmers could count on one rice harvest a
year and a few could also plant a crop of sweet potatoes or some
sugarcane. Since the introduction of the power tiller in 1959 (its
use presumes the availability of water), nearly all farmers can cultivate a second crop of sweet potatoes.

The Chianan system resulted in increased productivity and an
almost immediate rise in land value. Also increased was the number of land transactions. Land rarely changed hands in the pre-

Chianan period, and where land was sold it normally found its way into the hands of landlords. In 1929, 80 percent of all cultivating households in Chungshe were renting land; 44 percent were full tenants.[14] After completion of the Chianan system, however, a number of tenant farmers made use of increased earnings to buy land and the tenancy rate dropped off. On the eve of the Land-to-the-Tiller Program, the percentage of families tenanting some farmland had declined to 68.

Although absolute rent rose after completion of the Chianan system, the proportion of yield to rent declined. Tenants began to compete for more favorable fields in terms of the new water system, and landlords played tenants off against each other. For families cultivating rented land this was a period of great anxiety and insecurity. Since so many tenants were dependent upon landlords belonging to a single village lineage, antagonisms toward that group were exacerbated.

With the completion of the new irrigation system, water theft, previously rare, became a common phenomenon. Where soil and resources make it feasible, unauthorized water diversion has become institutionalized and thieves establish elaborate rotation schedules among themselves. Figure 2 suggests the extent of water theft in one typical "small area" in Chungshe. Actual plantings of rice during much of the period since 1930 have far exceeded official estimates. This excess area could have been irrigated only with water illegally diverted from the system. It should be noted that the mean hectarage cultivated by individual households in this area has steadily declined since 1935, and that the smaller a farmer's holding, the more likely he is to feel compelled to plant rice every year rather than rotating with sugarcane, in order to be sure of feeding his family. There are other reasons for the persistent preference for rice. Sugar prices have not always been stable; rice produces a crop in four months, whereas sugarcane takes eighteen; and the cultivation of rice allows more effective use of family labor during the year.

[14] Figures for 1929 were obtained from documents held by the Liuchia township office.

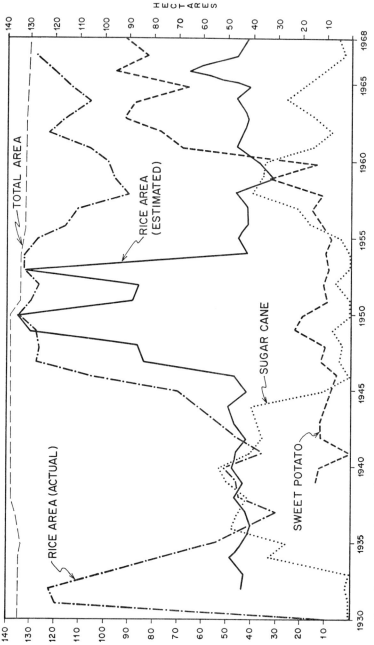

Fig. 2. Cropping patterns in a typical small area. The sharp increase in both estimated and actual plantings of rice that occurred after 1945 may reflect the removal of Japanese controls. The sharp drop in estimated plantings that occurred about 1954 may reflect a renewed attempt by the irrigation association to enforce the three-year rotation system (and a consequent unwillingness to give permission to farmers to grow rice out of turn) in the face of increased overall demand for water from the system. Sources: *Shui-tao tso-fu kwan-hsi shu-lei* (1930–37); *Pao-kao shu-chui Shui-tao tso-fu kwan-hsi shu-lei* (1937–47); *Chung-yao shu-lei* (1948–68)

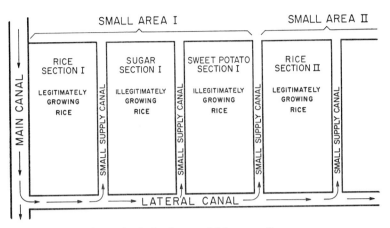

Fig. 3. An irrigation model for a small area.
Arrows indicate direction of water flow

As the potential for conflict over water has increased, means have evolved for managing or preventing disputes. The following cases will illustrate this.

Case 1. As noted above, small areas like the one schematically represented in Figure 3 are subdivided into three sections of about 50 hectares each. According to the rotation plan, each of the three sections should be cultivating a different crop, but all three are in fact growing rice. When a farmer in the section scheduled to grow sugarcane needs water, he watches the fields. Each farmer in the legitimate rice-growing section will come to his field shortly before his turn to draw water, so there will usually be at least one farmer there at any given time. The would-be thief will ask him whether he needs all the water he is entitled to, or whether he needs the entire period of his turn. If he does not, a small part of his share can be diverted through small ditches and drainages. When water is plentiful, the legitimate rice growers may not even bother to come to their fields early. In this case, the thief will simply divert water to meet his needs. Relations between farmers within the small area are face to face.

Case 2. Problems sometimes arise between small areas. Suppose, for example, that many farmers scheduled to grow sugarcane in Small Area I draw water out of turn. This will cause shortages farther down the line in Small Area II as the level of water in the lateral canal falls below that of the exit gates. Such a situation brings large blocs of farmers into opposition. But the customary way of handling the situation avoids violence by precluding the direct expression of hostility. One or more of the legitimate rice growers being deprived of water complain to the irrigation station. The clerk at the station telephones his counterparts at higher-level canal management stations. Water levels at each station—closely watched in any case to guard against theft—are checked until the diversion is located and corrected. Face-to-face encounters occur between agents of the irrigation association rather than between the two groups of farmers themselves. A potentially hostile situation is managed by taking it out of the hands of those directly involved in it.

Case 3. One night a certain Mr. Huang diverted water from an adjacent section of his small area into the supply canal leading to his field. Before it reached his field, however, this stolen water was diverted again, by a canal block placed by one Mr. Ts'ai. When Mr. Huang discovered the block, he went to work at once to remove it. Mr. Ts'ai saw him and came over to stop him. Mr. Huang complained that this was *his* stolen water. After some pushing and shoving, they finally agreed to take turns using the water. Mr. Huang was allowed to draw first.

Case 4. Eighteen farmers owning seven or eight hectares of land in a single section of the east Chungshe small area were all growing rice out of turn. Not enough water was available in their immediate vicinity, so they agreed to cooperate in drawing water illegally from a nearby lateral canal. A siphon was set up at point A on the Lin-feng-ying lateral canal (see Map 5). Water was lifted from the canal and led through a small drainage canal to the medium drainage canal indicated on the map. The medium canal was blocked at point B so that water south of the block would rise and flow southward (the reverse of normal flow in this canal). All

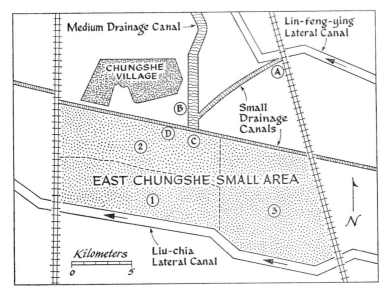

Map 5. A case of water theft in the east Chungshe small area.
Arrows in lateral canals show direction of water flow

who were to benefit from the diversion helped build the canal
block. A gas pump was installed at point C to lift water from the
medium drainage canal into a small drainage canal that ran along
the edge of the area to be watered. At point D the water was diverted by another block into the first field to be watered. From
there it was led to the other thieves' fields in a sequence previously agreed upon by all.

Farmers dependent on the medium drainage canal for irrigation
noticed that water had suddenly vanished from it. They immediately reported the fact to clerks of the irrigation association, who
eventually located the block and had it removed. Thus a conflict
was averted that might possibly have involved farmers in several
villages and might even have disrupted a large portion of the system. Violence was avoided by taking this potentially hostile situation out of the hands of those directly involved in it.

A number of technical considerations determine which farmers and how many farmers cooperate, how they steal water, and from where. Since the factors vary from year to year, the composition of stealing groups may also change. The fact that there are a great many ways to steal water means that there is also considerable variety in the potential sources of conflict. Thieving may involve the diversion of water from one section of a small area into another, or it can involve the diversion of water from one lateral canal into the area of another. In some situations water theft deprives only a few farmers of needed irrigation, in others it can bring farmers in different small areas into competition. In still other cases theft can generate conflicts between farmers on two lateral canals and lead to a potential confrontation between communities or entire regions. The extent and method of stealing and the nature of potential conflict are directly related to the availability of water, the location of water, and a number of other variable factors. But one thing is clear—where large numbers of farmers and vast areas of land are involved (actually or potentially) in a situation of conflict, simple cooperation on a face-to-face basis is no longer sufficient. In such situations a permanent managerial presence is required to articulate the interests of the groups concerned. The extension and integration of irrigation that occurred when the Chianan irrigation system was built required a parallel expansion of the cooperative and managerial networks previously developed by the farmers of the plain. Bernard Gallin (1966) has described the same sort of expansion in Hsin Hsing, another Taiwanese village. In that village, as in Chungshe, the extension of canal irrigation during the Japanese period made water available to a greater number of farmers, extended the area of interdependence, and broadened cooperative networks.

During the pre-Chianan period, farm families had to be largely self-sufficient with respect to labor; when it rained, all hands were needed at the same time for work on the family holdings. Labor peaks were intense but lasted only for short periods during the agricultural cycle. The larger areas under irrigation and the higher yields that became possible as a result of the new irrigation system served to increase overall labor needs. There was more rice to process. Since water was now intermittently supplied to the fields, at least three weedings were necessary, and on a larger area. Labor needs increased both in this area and in the coastal region, where rice could now be grown instead of sweet potatoes. At the same time, however, the availability of water spread this increased demand for labor over a longer period; liberated from their dependence on rainfall, farmers no longer had to act at the same time. Indeed, there is reason to believe that by blunting and extending peak periods of labor demand, the Chianan system may have removed an important impediment to family division. Before explaining why this should have been the case, let me introduce a few basic and necessary facts.

Rice nurseries are seeded from mid-May to mid-June, and the seedlings are ready 30 days later. Once the seedlings are ready, they must be transplanted within a period of twenty days. In the presence of heavy clay soils and a capricious water supply, it was imperative that fields be prepared no more than two or three days before transplanting. Premature preparation would give weed growth a head start and allow the soil to settle and harden so that it might be necessary to replow. We should also note that prior to the Second World War field labor in this Hokkien area consisted exclusively of males (many women had bound feet). With these facts in mind, consider the case of a model joint family and weigh the advantages and disadvantages of family division in terms of meeting labor needs. The family indicated in Figure 4 contains three males capable of field labor. It owns two buffalo and, like most families, cultivates about two hectares of land. Assuming an adequate water supply, this family would require nineteen to 22 days to prepare and transplant its holding. In other words. they could do the job within the twenty-day limit set by nature. But what if the brothers divided their family and holdings? Brother A, the eldest, would now have one buffalo, two workers, and one hectare of land. He could do the job in seventeen to twenty days. Brother B, alone with his buffalo, would need 23 to 26 days! He could not plant his entire area even given twenty days of sufficient moisture and even if he had prepared the first field to

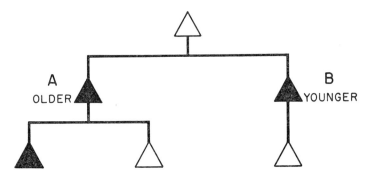

Fig. 4. A model joint family. Triangles designate males, solid triangles
males capable of field labor

be transplanted one or two days ahead. And this is assuming an adequate supply of water, which is not necessarily always forthcoming when rain is the only source. Brother B would be even worse off in a drought year. I am suggesting that we view the joint family in Chungshe at that time as an adaptation to crisis conditions. I think we see the justification for doing so even more convincingly when we consider situations in which the rice crop is lost.

There are two periods in the rice-growing cycle during which a crop can easily be lost. If, during the allowable twenty days for transplanting, there are fewer than fifteen days with sufficient water for preparing fields, the crops have to be abandoned. This was actually a frequent occurrence in Chungshe. Even more risky is the period just before and just after rice heading. If there is no substantial rain during a period of ten days before heading, or for a period of twenty days after, the crop is doomed. This was an even more common situation. If a farmer lost his rice, he would have to depend upon a crop of sweet potatoes to tide him over until the next year's rice harvest. But the clay soils prevalent in Chungshe are extremely difficult and time-consuming to open and prepare for sweet potatoes, particularly under drought conditions. Their poor drainage qualities also make them less suited for sweet potatoes than sandy soils would be. Each family tried to keep about .3 hectare of sandier soil within its holding as insurance against precisely such drought conditions.

Let us now assume that our model family has lost its rice. Its members have .3 hectare of sweet potatoes to live on for one year, which is barely enough to sustain them. They must plant the entire .3 hectare or borrow—or starve. As a joint family they could prepare and transplant their sweet potato crop, given seven sufficiently moist days. Working separately on divided plots, however, Brother A would need a total of eight sufficiently moist days to complete his .15 hectare and Brother B would need eleven days. And that is too much. In a drought year, according to my informants, a farmer could scarcely hope for more than seven sufficiently moist days between mid-August and the end of September. Even assuming the full seven days, Brother A could not quite plant his entire area, and Brother B would not come close. Only if they remained together could they plant the entire .3 hectare. This is an interesting predicament, especially since it is traditionally the wife of the younger brother in a Chinese joint family who is most eager to establish a separate household. She resents the fact that she and her husband are working to feed the unproductive children of her husband's older brother. In this situation, however, she and her husband would have least to gain from a family division.

With the completion of the Chianan system, water supplies became more continuous and dependable, labor became more readily available, and this particular obstacle to family division was removed. Rice is now a reliable crop, and sweet potato is no longer a crisis crop. I cannot demonstrate beyond all doubt that families in Chungshe actually delayed family division on the grounds just set forth; as we shall see in the following chapter, however, there is considerable demographic evidence to that effect.

Karl Wittfogel some years ago noted a propensity for nuclear as opposed to joint families in societies with large-scale irrigation (1935: 42–43, 48–49; or 1938: 7–8), and using data from 59 Indian villages, Henry Orenstein recently found statistical confirmation for the hypothesis that "villages which have more irrigation are the ones which have a lower percentage of joint families." Orenstein formulated two hypotheses that he proposed might constitute "an intervening variable between irrigation and the attenuation of the joint family." One was that "local territorially based

social groups will be weakened under the impact of irrigation,"
and that the weakening of such social groups would be manifested
in a dispersion of households. The second hypothesis was that
accompanying this dispersion of households would be a tendency
to weaken kinship based on groups such as the joint family.
Although neither of these hypotheses could be statistically vali-
dated, Orenstein felt that the effects of irrigation on the frequency of joint families could ultimately be related to the "immediate economic consequences" of irrigation (1956: 318–19):

Irrigation often accentuates the importance of cash crops and a money
economy. Where income is primarily for direct consumption, the joint
family stores its produce in one unit and uses it when needed. But when
a large part of income is in cash, its joint use becomes complicated, and
it is a fact that a number of joint families are divided because of quar-
rels over the disposition of money income.

Orenstein is probably on the right track in stressing the economic consequences of irrigation. With respect to the situation in
China, however, I suspect that a comparable focus on the divisive
effects of cash income would be too restrictive. Cohen's findings
(1967) and my own indicate that the need for labor and for an
efficient allocation of labor may play a greater role in determining family form than the simple presence or absence of cash income. Indeed, Cohen found the joint family thriving in association with tobacco growing (clearly a cash crop) in Yen-liao. As
he suggested, the real key to perpetuation of joint families probably lies in "the interdependent nature of the various economic
activities undertaken by different family members." More specifically, the joint form is likely to be retained where, in the event
of family partition, "the limited possibilities remaining to each
unit would not bring total returns as great as those derived from
the total investments of the family as now constituted," or where
"division would also mean a reduction in total income from present enterprises" (Cohen 1967: 642–43). The tenacity of joint families in pre-Chianan Chungshe would appear to represent a manifestation of these general principles.

Support for the suggestion that, in China at least, joint families are more likely to be found in unirrigated areas is to be found in data from John Lossing Buck's classic survey (1956). Buck indicates that only 16.6 percent of the crop area of China's wheat region (essentially north China) was under irrigation as opposed to 49.8 percent of the rice region (south China). The irrigated crop area of the rice region was thus nearly twice that of the wheat area (1956: 188). Buck also provides a table indicating the distribution of family members by relationship to family head for north and south China (1956: 367). According to his table, there were 27 percent more families containing head's brother in north China than in south China; 83 percent more with head's brother's wife; 100 percent more with head's brother's son; and 117 percent more with head's brother's daughter. These figures indicate not only that joint families are more likely to be found in north China than in south China, but also that the longer such families persist before partition the more likely they will be found in the north. Since Buck's figures on labor do not indicate with sufficient detail the distribution of need throughout the agricultural cycle, we cannot be sure that the intervening variable that I have suggested (i.e. labor need) was actually responsible for these differences. Still, Buck's figures are not inconsistent with this suggestion.

Irrigational modifications in Chungshe also had an effect upon demographic potentialities. As rice and sugarcane areas increased, the holding size necessary to maintain a family of six or seven (average for the time) decreased. This development was intensified by subsequent technological improvements in agriculture that served to increase yields. The result was that resources for a time permitted families to grow in size or to divide in accordance with ideal patterns of equal land inheritance. In terms of its high birthrate and adherence to the ideal of equal property inheritance, Chungshe village in the 1930's was adjusted to abundant land resources. Between 1935 and 1968, however, factors combined such that the high birthrate and household proliferation could no longer be sustained on the basis of compensatory increments in either land area or yield. Population has been slow in adjusting to these new restraints (witness the high birthrate in recent years

TABLE 11

Population Changes in Tatieh (1948–63) and Chungshe (1947–67)

	Tatieh				Chungshe			
Year	Births per 100	Deaths per 100	Population increase or decrease per 100	Net gain or loss through migration	Births per 100	Deaths per 100	Population increase or decrease per 100	Net gain or loss through migration
1947					6.54	3.86	+6.71	+4.03
1948	3.78	1.49	+1.97	−0.32	8.96	1.10	+8.64	+0.78
1949	4.40	1.47	+3.09	+0.16	6.80	1.88	+4.19	−0.73
1950	4.27	1.87	+2.02	−0.38	8.19	2.50	+3.05	−2.64
1951	3.74	1.17	+0.07	−2.50	7.28	2.02	+5.25	−0.01
1952	3.96	1.10	−0.29	−3.15	7.68	1.90	+0.76	−5.02
1953	5.08	1.69	+3.45	+0.06	9.28	1.52	+3.05	−4.71
1954	3.69	0.78	+2.77	−0.14	6.53	1.35	+0.86	−4.32
1955	4.15	1.17	+1.87	−1.11	10.27	1.34	+1.10	−7.83
1956	3.73	1.09	+1.69	−0.95	7.13	1.57	+3.38	−2.18
1957	3.41	0.94	−0.33	−2.80	6.90	1.16	−2.92	−8.66
1958	3.95	0.67	+1.94	−1.34	8.43	1.32	−0.36	−7.47
1959	3.09	0.79	+2.37	+0.07	7.98	1.33	+2.17	−4.48
1960	3.34	0.34	+1.09	−1.91	6.98	1.30	+7.92	+2.24
1961	2.60	0.63	+1.21	−0.76	7.52	1.75	+4.93	−0.84
1962	3.64	0.82	+3.89	+1.07	6.90	1.25	+3.55	−2.10
1963	2.96	0.72	+2.24	0.00	6.05	1.51	+2.01	−2.53
1964					4.74	0.89	+3.26	−0.59
1965					4.59	1.14	+5.65	+2.20
1966					5.44	0.81	+3.62	−1.01
1967					3.41	0.96	+5.59	+3.14
Mean	3.73	1.04	+1.81	−0.87	7.03	1.54	+3.44	−2.03

SOURCE: *Hu-chi t'ung-chi yüeh-pao piao* (Household register monthly statistical reports).

indicated in Table 11). The ideal of equal property inheritance is now rarely honored, and out-migration, a relatively recent phenomenon in the village, has intensified.

In the 33 years from 1935 to 1968, or about one and a half generations, the number of households in Chungshe doubled (see Table 12), and the mean size of holding decreased 44 percent, from about 2.5 hectares in 1935 to 1.4 hectares in 1968.[15] Since such a pattern might be expected if the average villager had two sons and divided his property equally between them, it appears

[15] In Tatieh, the mean size of holding decreased 33 percent, from 1.2 hectares in 1935 to only .8 hectare in 1964.

TABLE 12
Population and Households in Tatieh and Chungshe, 1920–68

Category	1920	1935	1964 (Tatieh) / 1968 (Chungshe)
Tatieh			
Number of households	148	189	265
Percent change		27.7%[a]	40.2%[b]
Population	809	1,051	1,602
Percent change		29.9%	52.4%
Chungshe			
Number of households	78	87	194
Percent change		11.5%	122.9%
Population	364	565	1,115
Percent change		55.2%	97.3%

SOURCE: Japanese censuses provided the figures for 1920 and 1935. The figures for 1964 and 1968 are based upon my own censuses and apply to units comparable to those of 1920 and 1935.

[a] Percentages in this column show changes from 1920 to 1935.

[b] Percentages in this column show changes from 1935 to 1964 (Tatieh) or 1968 (Chungshe).

that equal inheritance of land was practiced after 1935. Village informants confirm the fact.

In sum, then, Tatieh and Chungshe differ greatly with respect to the form of irrigation on which they depend, the way in which water is distributed and managed, the kinds of conflict that may arise, and the way in which such conflict is prevented and resolved. Starting from different points, the two villages were exposed to different irrigational pressures; and the ways they responded to these pressures were consequently different.

Labor. Because labor supply and demand have been so profoundly affected by changes in irrigation, most of my observations on labor in Chungshe have been presented in that connection. Certain other differences between the two communities with respect to the organization of labor have yet to be treated.

The composition of Chungshe's work teams indicates a greater tendency than in Tatieh for team leaders to solicit members who are close neighbors. In forming teams villagers also recognize the basic division of the community into "head" and "tail"; groups contain relatively few members from opposite sides of the village.

Team composition therefore reflects a basic social division within the community. Since agnates, especially in the village "head," are spatially concentrated, work teams on that side of the village normally include many such relatives. Generally speaking, teams in Chungshe contain many more agnates than those in Tatieh.

We have already noted the relationship in Chungshe between agnatic affiliation and neighborhood, especially in the village "head." Poorer villagers, representing a variety of surnames and living mainly in the village "tail," are more likely to contract marriages within the community. They frequently obtain spouses from families living in nearby compounds. On this side of the village, then, teams are more likely to contain a number of affines as well as agnates. The apparent preference for kinsmen could be a by-product of residential propinquity, yet the fact remains that the various work teams in Chungshe, unlike those in Tatieh, do manifest a kin-based commonality.

Capital and credit. The people of Chungshe borrow mainly to finance weddings and funerals, and secondarily to buy land or build houses. In the pre-Chianan period, borrowing was common because of the characteristic unreliability of crops and yields; many families had to borrow in dry years simply to keep themselves alive. Curiously enough, however, there are no institutions in Chungshe comparable to the *ku-hui*, or grain associations, of Tatieh, and villagers say there never have been any. Since such associations have been reported for many areas of Taiwan and the mainland, some explanation for their absence here seems called for.

Certain characteristics of the pre-Chianan period might have discouraged the appearance of grain associations. For one thing, until the introduction of the power tiller in the 1950's, most farmers continued to grow only one crop of rice a year; and the full year between harvests might have been too long a time for poor families to tie up capital in such societies. If a credit club has ten members, and if farmers, as in Tatieh, can count on two crops a year, then all members of the club would hold the fund as a lump sum within a period of five years. But where the cycle is only one year, fund rotation takes twice as long; moreover, a farmer who has to finance a wedding or funeral would have to wait a whole year to bid for the club fund and would be likely to seek help elsewhere. We should also recall that harvests in the pre-Chianan period were unreliable, so that in bad years villagers who had invested in a grain association would probably have found it necessary to borrow from other sources in any event. Other communities on the Chianan plain, to which these same inhibitory factors applied, seem also (to judge from the response to my inquiries) to have had no grain association.

Before credit became available through the farmers association, banks, and other such agencies, there were no sources of credit in Chungshe other than individual landlords, friends, and relatives. To this day, individuals constitute the main source of capital. Private loans carry rates of interest only slightly higher than agency loans, but they are easier to obtain and the terms of repayment can be more flexible. Landlords have always constituted the most important source of loans in the village. Although there were once a few nonkin associations in Chungshe from which one could borrow capital, such societies were fewer and poorer than their Tatieh counterparts. As in Tatieh, there is the feeling that one should not lend money to relatives if one can avoid it; and most people's relatives and close friends were in no position to lend money anyway. For most villagers, then, borrowing was from persons to whom one was not related.

The main landlords, hence the main lenders of money, were descendants of Lai Yüan, living in the village "head." There was thus a definite and widespread dependence on the patronage of members of this particular descent group, both for capital and for rented land. Landlords in Tatieh also constituted an important source of capital, but they were not associated with a single descent group or residential sector of the village. Thus, although access to loans in both communities has not been through agnates for most villagers, borrowing patterns in Chungshe, unlike those in Tatieh, contributed to the political and economic predominance of one agnatic group.

TABLE 13
Average Farm Earnings in Kaohsiung and Chianan in 1957
(*NT dollars*)

Item	Kaohsiung rice region (Tatieh)	Chianan mixed farming region (Chungshe)
Farm receipts[a]		
Average for all size holdings	19,832	17,388
For average holding in Tatieh/Chungshe[b]	17,112	17,322
Farm expenditures[c]		
Average for all size holdings	10,685	10,171
For average holding in Tatieh/Chungshe	9,516	10,159
Farm earnings		
Average for all size holdings	9,147	7,217
For average holding in Tatieh/Chungshe	7,596	7,163

SOURCE: Y. C. Tsui, *A Summary Report on Farm Income of Taiwan in 1957 in Comparison with 1952* (Taipei, JCRR Economic Digest Series, no. 13, 1959, p. 47).
[a] Includes receipts from crops, livestock, poultry, and others.
[b] Includes expenditures for feeds, fertilizers, seed, seedlings, taxes, man labor, livestock expenses, land rent or interest, depreciation, etc.
[c] Average holding in 1960 for Tatieh was .83 hectares and for Chungshe 1.31 hectares. The JCRR report provides figures for holdings of .50–.99 and 1.00–1.99 hectares, which we adopt here.

Yields and incomes. We have compared Tatieh and Chungshe in terms of their major resources. Let us now consider the proceeds that farmers in each village extract from these assets, specifically yields and incomes. Although Tatieh appears to be better off than Chungshe from the point of view of soil, yield per hectare, number of crops grown, and availability of irrigation water, the larger number of households dependent on cultivation in Tatieh cancels out these advantages. Table 13 provides figures on farm income and expenditure for the "Kaohsiung rice region" and the "Chianan mixed farming region" in 1957. These figures were obtained in the course of a survey conducted by the Sino-American Joint Commission on Rural Reconstruction. The figures on farm income do not radically differ from those resulting from our own calculations if we control on average holding size. According to the survey figures on farm expenditures, the average holding in Tatieh required a lower expenditure than that in Chungshe. The result is that farm earnings turn out to be marginally higher in the Kaohsiung region. These calculations all suggest that average farm earnings in Tatieh and Chungshe were not radically different during the period 1957–60.

It is likely that average farm income in Tatieh has increased somewhat more dramatically than in Chungshe in recent years, owing to the increasing acreage given to bananas (a cash crop) in that village since 1963. It should also be noted that prior to 1930, when a single crop of rice could be grown in Chungshe only during years of adequate rainfall, yields were reportedly very low. Droughts were not infrequent, and farmers at such times had to depend entirely on sweet potatoes to tide themselves over until better times. Prior to 1930, then, Tatieh villagers seem to have been considerably better off as a group than Chungshe villagers.

THREE

Kinship

A<small>T THE TIME</small> of my field study in Chungshe, the distribution of family forms was similar to that in Tatieh a few years earlier. In 1968, 96 percent of all Chungshe households were either stem or nuclear families; 91 percent of all Tatieh households took one of these two forms in 1964. The median household size in both villages was 6.0 persons. From a historical and dynamic point of view, however, there have been significant differences in the trends affecting family form in each community. Before 1930, as we have seen, there were forces at work in Chungshe that inhibited the expression of fissive tendencies within the family, tendencies that apparently were not so effectively thwarted in Tatieh and elsewhere in China. Those forces evidently ceased to exist after 1930, and a rapid breakdown of complex families took place.

Tatieh and Chungshe also differ with respect to the way in which mates and adopted sons are obtained. In both communities, marriage alliances are seen in instrumental terms and valued for broadening the range of affinal ties; but Tatieh villagers frequently select spouses from within the community—a pattern rare in Chungshe and in China generally. Also significant is the fact that adopted sons, who are often essential to ensure family continuity, are more commonly obtained from agnates in Chungshe than in Tatieh.

Some of the most interesting and important differences between Tatieh and Chungshe occur in the area of agnatic affiliation beyond the family. Most striking in this regard is the persistence in Chungshe of corporate lineages. These lineages have far less impressive assets than many lineages in southeastern China, but they have displayed greater viability and structural elaboration than their counterparts in Tatieh, and they resemble more closely the Confucian model of a strong, localized descent group. In Chungshe patrilineal affiliation has provided an important basis for collective action, whereas in Tatieh it was by playing down agnatic affiliation that villagers managed to achieve a higher degree of community integration. Because the internal and external requirements of villagers in these two communities were dissimilar, the kinds of agnatic structures they developed have also been different.

TATIEH

The network of people to whom a family in Tatieh may turn for help and support is broadened through marriage.[1] Affines represent a potential source of temporary labor, and villagers in need of capital sometimes invite them to participate in grain associations. Through affines pressure can often be exerted at various levels of the official hierarchy and voters may be influenced during elections. Due consideration must therefore be given to the political and economic potentialities of families from which spouses are taken. Once established, affinal ties are carefully maintained and periodically reinforced. Visits and gifts are exchanged, and reciprocal participation in ceremonies (e.g. marriages, birthdays, funerals, feasts) is expected. Once the linkage on which an affinal tie is based exceeds two ascending generations, however, reciprocity relationships are less likely to be maintained.

Marriage and affinal relations. A number of customary restrictions on the selection of spouses serve to encourage a broad ramification of affinal ties. Marriage with first or second cousins, for example, is frowned on, with the result that families already linked by marriage within three generations are automatically excluded from consideration as potential sources of spouse.[2] Levi-

[1] The functional importance of affinal relatives in Chinese society has already been underscored by a number of writers (e.g. Lin 1948; Fried 1953; Freedman 1958; and Gallin 1960).

[2] The only type of cousin marriage tolerated is between matrilateral parallel cousins (i.e. with mother's sister's daughter). The two such marriages that took

TABLE 14

Marriages in Tatieh by Origin of Spouse, 1959–64

Place of origin	Brides	Grooms
Hsinpi township:		
Tatieh village	26	26
Other villages	4	3
Wanluan township	4	0
Neipu township	3	1
Chiatung township	12	6
Chutien township	2	1
Other	3	17
TOTAL	54	54

SOURCE: The figures, for January 1959 through August 1964, are based on household interviews. Their accuracy is confirmed by the household register for Tatieh village.

rate and sororate marriages, another way of repeating affinal ties already established, are also considered unacceptable. In positive terms, villagers consistently prefer women from within the village or from a particular constellation of neighboring Hakka communities (see Table 14). Agnatic connections tracing back to the mainland and cooperation (especially for defense) have linked these communities from the time of their settlement. Japanese household registers and my own genealogical reconstructions suggest that before 1945 there was an even greater tendency for marriages to be arranged in accordance with these priorities. In recent years, wider contacts have provided somewhat greater choice.

It is significant that 48 percent of all brides and an equal percentage of grooms married in Tatieh in 1959–64 were residents of the village. This high percentage runs counter to patterns described for other areas of China.[3] Not only do neighbors marry in Tatieh, but also, as the following examples show, procedural

place in Tatieh in recent years both ended in separation, and villagers point to these cases as vivid proof that cousin marriage is unwise.

[3] See Pratt (1960: 151–52), M. Yang (1948: 115–16), and C. K. Yang (1959b: 84–85). Reluctance to marry within the community presumably reflects an emphasis on patrilineal as against affinal bonds. According to Pratt (1960: 152), "The role of a wife in China demands that she shall sever all jural connections with her family at marriage, and it appears that, without actual formulation, the preferred distance should be just too far for a woman to be able to run home after disputes in her husband's family."

distinctions between affinally related families during wedding ceremonies are less clearly drawn than elsewhere.[4] We have observed that economic activity in Tatieh demands considerable cooperation within the village across agnatic boundaries. It seems clear that the way family ceremonial activities are handled reflects the important role of affines and friends in village life in general.

Ceremonial behavior. On the day before a villager's wedding, he normally carries sacrifices to his mother's ancestral hall and to the hall of his paternal grandmother. On the wedding day, the groom's feast is attended not only by his family members, close agnates, and friends, but by many of his bride's kinsmen and family friends as well. Tables for the bride's company are set apart, but there is ample time and opportunity for socializing between the groups. On the day after the wedding it is customary for the new couple to return to the bride's home for a second feast, and the groom is accompanied at this time by a number of his kinsmen and friends. Once again affinal groups feast and socialize together. Other details of the wedding similarly indicate extensive involvement with affines. In Tatieh—unlike, for example, Taitou (cf. M. Yang 1948: 110)—a groom is required to join his bride in worshiping her ancestors when he goes to claim her. During the wedding ceremonies a male child of the bride's natal family offers incense on their behalf in the groom's ancestral hall. The ceremony of *p'eng-ch'a*, "offering tea," is performed by the groom in the ancestral hall of his bride as well as by the bride in his ancestral hall. Both occasions are used to introduce the new spouse to his or her relatives through marriage and to the friends of these relatives.[5]

[4] A number of writers have stressed the fact that marriage rituals and associated ceremonies in China vividly symbolize the separation of a woman from her natal family and her integration into the family of her husband (see C. K. Yang 1959b: 83; and Freedman 1970: 184).

[5] In Nanching, by contrast, as described by C. K. Yang, "there was no part of the traditional marriage procedure in which the two families gathered together for any kind of common celebration" (1959a: 26; cf. Pratt 1960: 153). Something like the Tatieh pattern was found by Freedman among the Chinese of Singapore (1957: 76): "The structure of the local kindred shows a shift of emphasis away from the strong patrilineal bias of the home kindred. Going out in marriage does not have for the Singapore Chinese girl the exclusive sense it

No household has sufficient labor to carry out the elaborate preparations required during family-sponsored feasts. Outdoor ovens must be built, tables and dishes fetched and cleaned, animals and poultry slaughtered, food cooked, canopies erected, invitations printed and sent out, etc. Where 20 or 30 tables are provided to feast 150 to 250 guests, 20 or 30 men and women may be called upon to assist. Preparations usually take several days, during which time helpers must be fed. Studies of labor use during five weddings revealed that unrelated neighbors and relatives through marriage constituted a greater proportion of the total labor force than agnates. Assistance provided on the occasion of birthday, birth, or wedding feasts constitutes more than a spontaneous manifestation of altruism. It rises out of an ongoing system of reciprocal obligations, the existence of which guarantees that no family will be unable to fulfill its ceremonial responsibilities because of a labor deficiency. Those who provide assistance are usually also involved in cooperation more directly related to subsistence.

Wedding, birth, and birthday celebrations have in common the fact that they are joyous events that may be planned for in advance. Financing can be arranged over a long period, and helpers can be recruited long before the event takes place. A considerable portion of the work can be accomplished by the host family and close agnates. Funerals, on the other hand, often impose sudden and unexpected demands, particularly when death strikes in the middle of a harvest season, when friends and relatives are busy. The immediate relatives of the deceased are expected to be too grief-stricken to contribute their labor during most of these preparations. The *fu-mu hui*, or "father-mother association" (there are at least ten in Tatieh), is tailored to meet the particular requirements that arise from death; membership in such funeral associations guarantees against labor deficiencies. Villagers join them to ensure that ritual obligations will be fulfilled upon the death of their parents, or as a guarantee against the time of their own passing. Each father-mother association consists of 28, 32, or 36

---

carried in the village life of China. She may be leaving home, but she is not being extruded from a territorially compact bloc of kinsmen."

TATIEH, FIRST FOUR PAGES
Above: Aerial view of Tatieh
Below: Women of Tatieh

Above: Detail of temple roof
Below: Arrival of the bride

Above: The Ghost Festival
Right: God's medium

Above: Procession to the cemetery
Right: Funeral ritual

CHUNGSHE, NEXT FOUR PAGES
Above: Main street
Below: Itinerant fishmonger

Above: Chungshe's temple
Right: Man of the village "tail"

Above: The Sungchiang Society
Left: The Festival of Buddha
procession

Funeral ritual

members. When the society is organized, each participant contributes 30 catties of rice to a common fund. Group assets are used to buy tables, chairs, and other equipment necessary for the funeral feast. Liquid assets are loaned to association members at moderate rates of interest. Meetings are convened twice a year, after each rice harvest, at which time loans are extended or repaid. When funerals have been provided for all members, the association's remaining assets are distributed among the descendants and it is dissolved.

The funeral society goes into action immediately upon receiving word that a death has occurred. Each member proceeds to the home of the deceased with an obligatory contribution of polished rice. The society assumes responsibility for printing and delivering death notices, calling the various funeral specialists, ordering the coffin, digging the grave, erecting canopies and funeral altars, and preparing the feast. The immediate family of the deceased is responsible for paying all costs, but the father-mother association makes most of the arrangements. Its members are continuously involved in assisting the funeral specialists at their various tasks. Altars must be erected, moved, and modified. Tables must be set up and taken down. The wives of association members sew mourning garments and help prepare the feast. After funeral ceremonies have been completed, members of the association carry the coffin to the cemetery and bury it.

Since members of a father-mother association are too occupied during the funeral to wail for the deceased, they should not be too closely related to him. During funeral proceedings sons and grandsons, along with their wives, form the main core of wailers; along with unmarried daughters and granddaughters and the sons and unmarried daughters of brothers, these relatives should be free, so far as possible, of routine duties during the funeral. It follows that brothers, and even patrilateral first cousins and second cousins, are infrequently found in the same father-mother association. Indeed most members are either not unrelated or only distantly related; the main tie between them is not agnation but friendship. As the preface to the organization book of one association states, "Mutual aid in funerary matters is related to the joy and sorrow of friends." People who cooperate at such times are likely to be people who frequently cooperate in a variety of sub- sistence-related activities.[6]

Ceremonial feasts attract guests and provide an opportunity to renew and revitalize old ties. On each occasion a list of guests is maintained in which gifts brought are clearly and precisely recorded.[7] From a comparison of guests lists and several on-the- spot observations, some general conclusions about the kinds of people who attend these affairs are possible. Invariably, agnates of the host constitute a minority of all guests. At a feast given by an average farming family with relatively few outside contacts, many guests will be relatives through marriage and many others will be fellow villagers. If the host or one of his family members has received a formal education beyond elementary school or works outside the village, most guests are likely to be unrelated friends from other communities and relatives through marriage.

Family perpetuation. Marriage is the link between past and future generations, the means by which a family line can be pro- jected one more step. Tatieh villagers share with Chinese every- where the conviction that bearing an heir is an obligation owed to past generations; it is having a son that allows a married couple to take their rightful place in adult society. When it becomes apparent that a couple cannot themselves provide an heir, there- fore, the problem of family continuity must be resolved some other way. The usual course is adoption.[8]

[6] The funeral societies described here differ in certain respects from those described by Kulp (1925: 196–203). Tatieh villagers do not join funeral associ- ations for essentially financial reasons, or to ensure a respectable number of wailers; wailers are in any event close relatives and thus rarely members of the same funeral association. They join primarily to be sure of commanding an adequate labor force when death strikes. At the same time, membership reinforces other kinds of cooperation between unrelated families. It should perhaps be noted that the basically nonagnatic character of the funeral asso- ciation in Tatieh is not unique to that village (see Freedman 1958: 94); the point is simply that where both options exist—as they do not, for example, in a single-lineage village—the nonagnatic option has been taken.

[7] The host is expected to reciprocate when each guest provides a similar feast, and these lists provide a guideline for determining an appropriate gift on such occasions.

[8] Despite the compulsion for begetting heirs, few villagers chose to resolve

Ideally, sons should be adopted from close agnates. I was frequently told that the sons of one's brother are preferred because "they are of the same blood," or because "fertilized water should not be allowed to flow into outside streams." Genealogical reconstructions, interviews, and materials contained in the household registers revealed twenty resident villagers who had at some time been adopted sons. Expressed preferences notwithstanding, in only three instances were adopted sons actually obtained from patrilineal relatives of the foster parents. Relatives through marriage and unrelated persons were a far more important source.[9]

Where parents have given birth to daughters but no sons, the problem of family continuity may be resolved by an arrangement known as *chao-hsü*, or "calling a son-in-law." In such instances the groom agrees to take up residence with his wife's family and to allow at least one of his sons to bear her surname. A man who marries in this fashion is said to *ju-chui*, or "enter the family of his wife." The term *chui* (parasite) suggests the character of such an act and reflects the low esteem with which villagers view such marriages. A girl's family is not likely to "call a son-in-law" unless it can provide no heir by natural or adoptive means; the groom's family will agree to such an arrangement only in return for some definite material advantage or where the alternative is poverty. An uxorilocal husband is rarely expected to produce an engagement gift. In addition, he gains access to the property of his in-laws and relieves pressure upon his own family's resources. The fact that seven resident villagers had married in this way may testify to the difficulties involved in obtaining sons by adoption.

Recent trends. In recent years the family has been exposed to the working of new forces. Young people are becoming less dependent on the family estate and its head, and have new ideas about

---

problems of apparent infertility by taking a *hsiao-chieh*, or concubine. According to my records, only three men now have concubines. Aside from the economic disadvantages of having to support many dependents, villagers frown on such arrangements because of the conflicts they cause within the family.

[9] Out of seventeen cases, I am certain that at least ten sons were adopted from relatives by marriage. Daughter adoption is also quite common; my studies revealed a total of 21 resident villagers who had at some time been adopted daughters. In no instance was an adopted daughter obtained from an agnate.

the goals of marriage and the objectives of family life. An important factor in this changing attitude has been the greater availability of outside employment. As population pressure grows, the possibilities of continued land division become restricted and families find it difficult to make optimum use of all household labor on the farm. Many try to keep the family farm intact by directing the energies of some members to occupations off the farm. The land situation is aggravated by the fact that few landowners are now willing to become landlords. As we noted earlier, recent agrarian policies have rendered tenanted land unprofitable as well as difficult to recover and sell. As a result, farmers who hope to augment inadequate holdings or replace lost ones by becoming tenants have little chance of success.[10]

Opportunities to supplement family income through seasonal or permanent employment in the immediate vicinity are limited. In fact, their number has declined since 1945 thanks to the increasing mechanization of work in the fields of the sugar refinery in nearby Nanchou. Thus a worsening man-land ratio, combined with limited possibilities for supplementing family income by employment in or near the village, forces many young men to leave home in search of work.[11]

Another factor in changing the attitudes of young people has been the gradual expansion of education. Before 1895 access to formal education was essentially confined to a few wealthy families of various surnames, who jointly engaged a teacher to drum the

[10] In 1952 only six households were cultivating no land; by 1964 the number had risen to 44. An even greater number of households supplement their farm-derived income with income from full- or part-time work off the farm. In 1964, 78 percent of all village households had one or more resident members engaged in such work, most of it (48 percent of households) on a full-time basis. About 58 percent of all households derived at least part of their total annual income from salaries and wages.

[11] Calculations based on township records indicate an average net annual loss of registered population through out-migration of .87 percent between 1947 and 1963. Since villagers frequently leave home for extended periods without altering their household registration, the total registered population in any given year is likely to exceed the population actually resident in the village. For this reason, .87 percent should be considered a minimum estimate of population loss through migration.

TABLE 15

Level of Education in Tatieh, 1947 and 1960

(Percent)

Level of formal education	1947			1960		
	Male	Female	Both	Male	Female	Both
Elementary	46.8%	30.2%	38.5%	52.9%	49.9%	51.4%
Lower middle	7.0	3.2	5.1	11.9	6.4	9.1
Upper middle	1.5	.6	1.1	7.1	1.6	4.4
College	.8	0	.4	1.1	0	.6
TOTAL	56.1%	34.0%	45.1%	73.0%	57.9%	65.5%

SOURCE: *Hsien-chü jen-k'ou chiao-yü ch'eng-tu* (Educational level of resident population).

classical texts into their children. Under the Japanese, the curriculum was altered and the number of students gradually expanded, and since 1945 public education has become virtually universal on Taiwan. Tatieh villagers are much better educated now than they were at the end of the Japanese occupation (see Table 15).

The expansion of formal education, particularly beyond the elementary school level, means that more young people in the village are qualified for occupational opportunities opening up outside the village. As they capitalize on these opportunities, they become less bound to the family estate and its head. In middle school lasting friendships are formed that ramify well beyond the community and even beyond the ethnic group. These relationships are maintained and reinforced through such mechanisms as periodic meetings of former classmates and exchanges of visits. The increasing role played by young people in politics and economic affairs may be partially attributed to their wider range of contacts. Not only are they less dependent on their parents in their quest for jobs, spouses, and support, but they are increasingly in a position to help their parents as a result of their personal contacts, for example in obtaining private loans and temporary workers. Similarly, candidates running for office are eager to recruit young men as their linemen, or persuaders.

Since 1945, "Western" notions regarding the family, as relayed in novels, films, and radio programs, have become increasingly prominent in the countryside. Until the end of the Japanese period, marriages continued to be arranged according to the discretion of parents. Where spouses came from different communities, the groom frequently saw his bride for the first time on the day of his wedding. Although marriages are still formally arranged by parents, young people tend more and more to choose their own partners, and marriage is often preceded by a period of dating. Younger parents approve of this development. "It is not enough," as one villager put it, "to see a prospective bride standing in a doorway with half her face hidden behind the door. Who knows if she has an eye on the side you cannot see?" Premarital dating also removes a burden of guilt from the parents should the marriage later turn sour.

Older villagers, by contrast, frequently complain that family solidarity is weakening as a result of recent developments. In particular, they assert that daughters-in-law, being more secure in their conjugal relationships and better educated than their parents-in-law, tend to be disrespectful and to flaunt their independence. They resist hard work, visit their natal homes too frequently, and demand far too much attention from their husbands.

Family form and family division. The joint family is a brittle social unit; it may work for a while, but normally tensions within it soon lead to a family division. Family estates can be partitioned, and households divided, either in piecemeal fashion or all at once. One brother at a time may demand his share, or all may participate in the division simultaneously. Whichever procedure is used, a division of estate alters the fraternal relationship. The ideal outcome of family partition is a division of the estate into equivalent shares. The parents retain one share for themselves and take up residence with their favorite son (regardless of his birth order). When they die, their share is divided among their sons, who jointly finance all funeral expenses. Where space permits, partitioning brothers set up separate kitchens in the same compound. Although their budgets and holdings have been divided, they continue to cooperate in a number of ways so long as friendly relations con-

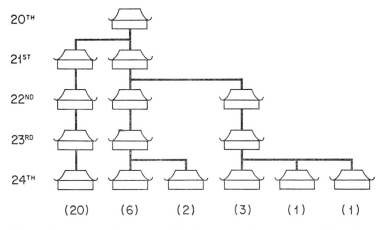

Fig. 5. Fissioning of compound halls among the progeny of Liu Ying-p'iao. Figures at left are generations. Figures at bottom indicate number of households using each hall in 1968

tinue to exist between them. The compound ancestral hall is held as common property, and the costs of maintaining it are jointly shared. Divided families continue to worship in the same hall, but their daily offerings are now made independently.

In the event that brothers do not remain on good terms, or when a new compound is constructed, a separate ancestral hall may be built and a new ancestral tablet lodged in it. There is no prohibition against the multiplication of ancestral tablets, and newer ones are often more impressively fabricated and more comprehensive in terms of genealogical depth than the originals. Hakka ancestral tablets list ancestors representing many generations, along with a general reference to all unnamed ancestors (cf. Freedman 1958: 81–84; and Freedman 1970). Their form and treatment reflect the autonomous character of newly established ancestral halls. When two brothers part and one builds a new hall complete with tablet, ritual cooperation between them is greatly reduced. It is worth noting that although most Liu households in Tatieh are the descendants of a single ancestor who arrived in the village some 150 to 200 years ago, the Liu now worship in six separate ancestral halls (see Fig. 5). There is no ritual nesting such that persons who worship in one hall periodically also worship in a higher-level hall.

Brothers who have partitioned may be conceived of as a minimal corporate lineage in the sense that they own certain things jointly (e.g. the ancestral hall). Except for certain mutual ceremonial obligations, the extent to which they cooperate depends on the nature of their relationship. Brothers who are on good terms may lend each other tools, drying grounds, buffalo, or small amounts of money, or exchange labor for relatively small jobs. Where factional disputes exist with other families, brothers may find themselves involved in a degree of political cooperation as well. But where family division results from or leads to conflict, the parties commonly have more intensive reciprocity relationships with unrelated households or families related by marriage.

Other things being equal, fraternal obligations take precedence over those associated with friendship. Other things are rarely equal, however, and where conflicts arise between obligations to close agnates and obligations to close but unrelated friends, resolutions differ.[12] The claim exerted by agnatic bonds on personal loyalties also weakens in proportion to genealogical and residential distance.

Agnatic kinship beyond the family. In 1964 there were only five corporate lineages (beyond the level of divided brothers sharing a compound ancestral hall) in Tatieh village. One of these was formed as late as 1953. Only three possessed a landed estate, their combined holdings amounting to only 3.5 hectares. The two remaining groups held no corporate real estate but did possess small funds that were used to finance joint sacrificial rites and to provide small loans to group members.

The Liu-ming ancestral trust is of particular interest. With twenty households owning shares in it (all of which worship in the same ancestral hall), the Liu-ming corporation is the largest in Tatieh. It was first established about 150 years ago, and was sub-

[12] The data from Tatieh support Fried's contention (1953: 67) that in China "friendship is not merely a supplement to relationship based on kinship. It is an authentic field of intercourse in its own right. Though, at times, it serves as a complement to pre-existing kinship rights and obligations it often challenges kinship for prior loyalty."

sequently dissolved during the Japanese occupation. In 1953, three of Liu-ming's descendants contributed to the creation of a new Liu-ming ancestral trust. The assets of this corporation, now amounting to approximately 8,000 catties of unhusked rice, are lent out at interest.

The earnings of the corporation are used as follows. Approximately 650 catties of unhusked rice are set aside each year to pay for the *Ch'ing-ming* (Festival of Graves) sacrifice presented before the tomb of Liu-ming, and to finance an annual lineage feast. The management of these undertakings and responsibility for maintaining the ancestral hall rotate annually among the twenty households owning shares in the corporation.[13] A representative of each member household attends the annual feast, during which any remaining profits are distributed as follows: (1) NT$100 to all males over 60 years, (2) NT$50 to all females over 60, (3) one peck of unhusked rice to each male born during the previous year, (4) one peck of unhusked rice to each daughter married during the previous year, and (5) 100 catties of unhusked rice reserved for maintenance of the ancestral hall.

The Chiu ancestral corporation includes fifteen households, all of which worship in a common ancestral hall. This lineage, reportedly also established about 150 years ago, no longer owns any cultivated land. The entire estate consists of 6,500 catties of unhusked rice, lent to members at interest. The profits from this trust are distributed in much the same fashion as those from the Liu-ming trust.

There are two separate and distinct Lai ancestral trusts to which Tatieh families belong. The Lai Kuo-ta estate was established during the early years of the Japanese occupation. Nine households, only one of which still resides in Tatieh, currently enjoy access to this estate. Half a hectare of land is rented out, and the profits are enjoyed by each shareholding household on a rotational basis. No

13 Rotation in this particular case is on a household rather than lineage-branch basis. The egalitarian way in which this estate is handled has prompted some members to suggest that this organization is not properly a lineage corporation at all.

TABLE 16

Ownership of Land in Tatieh in 1935

Type of owner	Hectares	Percent
Individuals:		
Absentee (Hokkien) landlords	82	39%
Tatieh villagers	44	21
TOTAL	126	60%
Lineages:		
With village members	36	17%
Without village members	12	6
TOTAL	48	23%
Associations:		
With village members	28	13%
Without village members	8	4
TOTAL	36	17%
GRAND TOTAL	210	100%

SOURCE: Data contained in the *Ti-tsu ming-chi chang* (Land tax record), volume for Tatieh village.

annual meetings, sacrifices, or celebrations are held. Five households are nominal members of the Lai Mu-ch'iu trust, which technically owns two hectares of land in a neighboring township. Thanks to a series of misfortunes, a public school came to be built upon this land, with the result that it yields no profits of any sort and the corporation has effectively ceased to exist.

Thus in 1964 some 19 percent of all village households owned shares in functioning lineage corporations, whose total assets amounted to only 1.5 hectares of profit-producing land and some 14,500 catties of rice. Things were strikingly different in earlier years. In 1935, according to Japanese tax records, lineages owned about 23 percent of all private farmland in Tatieh (see Table 16); at roughly the same time, if my calculations are correct (Table 17), villagers participated in 21 lineage corporations with assets of 134 hectares (located in and out of the village). The absence of highly developed corporate lineages in Tatieh today does not mean that distant patrilineal ties have lost all functional importance. But the erosion of this symbol of their strength in only thirty years is striking enough to warrant an effort at explanation.

TABLE 17
Number and Land Holdings of Corporate Lineages and
Associations to Which Tatieh Villagers Belonged, 1935–64

Year	Association[a]		Corporate lineages	
	Number	Hectares	Number	Hectares
1935	31	97	21	134
1952	5	52	6	4
1964	1	17	5	3

SOURCE: *Shōmei ni kansuru shōrui tetsu* (Collections of evidential documents), vols. 2–14, 1927–39; *Ti-tsu ming-chi chang* (Land tax record), for Tatieh, Chienkung, Hsinpi, Chutien, and Wanluan; *Ch'i-shui cheng-shou teng-chi pu* (Contract tax collection register); and the *Ti-t'u fu-chi ts'e na-shui jen-hsing ming-so yin* (Land tax taxpayer's name index). The profile obtained from documentary sources was modified and corrected in accordance with information provided by informant interviews.

[a] Only associations with a corporate focus in land are included.

Certain characteristics usually associated with strong lineage organization are absent from any of Tatieh's lineages. On the basis of materials from southeastern China, Maurice Freedman has suggested a relationship between stratification and lineage strength (1958: 126):

It seems on the whole that the larger lineages were the more highly differentiated internally in terms of social status.... What probably happened in essence was that social differentiation and growth in numbers were constantly reinforcing each other. Increasing differentiation in status brought benefits to the lineage as a whole which provided incentives for people to stay within it.

There is no indication that descent groups in Tatieh were ever characterized by a high degree of internal social or economic differentiation. For example, none of them owned ancestral temples (as distinct from compound halls). The high cost of building such an edifice can only be afforded by families or groups of families with above average assets. The hierarchical nesting of corporate lineage branches, taken by Freedman (1958: 46–50) as a manifestation of socioeconomic differentiation, was never more than rudimentary in Tatieh. Where more inclusive corporations did exist, they were invariably produced by the aggregation of branches in the different communities (cf. Pasternak 1968a, 1968b, and 1969). About 140 years ago, for example, a certain Hsü Kuang-ming

established an ancestral estate in Wanluan consisting of ten hectares. The trust was specifically set aside to provide for his own
worship after death, and access to its profits was to be enjoyed only
by his descendants. He later contributed to the establishment of
another ancestral estate, consisting of four hectares, for the worship of his great-grandfather. Hsü families in many other Hakka
villages on the plain also contributed to the endowment of this
ancestral trust, and a corporate focus for agnates and collaterals
living in a number of communities was thus created. In Tatieh
alone, three collateral Hsü lines with separate corporate foci were
united by this trust with each other and with families in other
communities. Cohen describes lineage corporations among Hakka
in Meinung, noting a similar merging process (1969: 177–81).

Many Hakka on the Pingtung plain who bear the surname Ch'en
and trace their origins to Chiaying *chou* in Kwangtung are gene-
alogically divided into several *hu*, or sublineages. Most of Tatieh's
Ch'en belong to a sublineage known as Nan-shan, or "South
Mountain." As in the case of Hsü, Nan-shan Ch'en living in various villages were united by the creation of two ancestral trusts
with headquarters in Chutien township. One included all descendants of the Nan-shan first ancestor; the second was limited
to descendants of the third ancestor. During the 1920's, both corporations contributed funds to establish an estate and construct a
clan association temple in Pingtung city.[14] Shareholders in either
of the two founding lineages were entitled to a proportionate
number of shares in the new clan association. In addition, any
Ch'en who paid to have his private ancestral tablet installed in
the temple was entitled to a specified number of shares. Finally,
any person with the surname Ch'en who contributed the price of
one share could become a member of the clan association.

If Tatieh villagers belonged to large, inclusive descent groups,
then, these were the products of aggregation rather than segmentation. In all cases their headquarters were located outside the

---

[14] Membership in a clan association, in contrast to membership in a corporate lineage, does not require an ability to demonstrate common descent. It is
normally sufficient to simply stipulate common descent on the basis of having
a common surname. For a discussion of clan associations on Taiwan, see Fried
(1966).

village. Neither aggregation nor segmentation produced nested lineage corporations within the community itself. Where relatively poor agnatic corporations are merged by the creation of more inclusive units, the nesting pattern that results cannot be thought of as a manifestation of socioeconomic stratification. Indeed, informants testify to the relative lack of stratification in Tatieh, at least during the Japanese period. All villagers personally worked the land, and there were no great differences in life style. Within the community there were no big landlords, nor did any village landlords move to town houses. Although villagers were certainly not equal in terms of wealth, education, or political influence, there were apparently no bona fide "country gentlemen." As far as I can determine, no villager ever passed a Ch'ing civil service examination.

Given this low degree of stratification, what incentives were there for Tatieh villagers to cling to their lineages or to emphasize agnatic bonds? According to Freedman (1958: 127),

The essential feature of land tenure in Fukien and Kwangtung was the important role ascribed to the corporate holdings of lineages and their segments. When the landlord was often the agnatic group of which the tenant was a member, and when being a member of such a group meant having a prior right to tenancy, the poorer people had every reason to stay in the community rather than go to try their luck elsewhere.... When corporate land was either rented out to members of the corporation or circulated for use among them, the privilege proved a centripetal force.

Not all the lineage-owned land in Tatieh was owned by agnatic groups to which villagers belonged, and only seventeen of the 21 lineages to which they did belong in 1935 owned land in Tatieh. The total area amounted to only 17 percent of all farmland in the village. The remaining 6 percent of lineage-owned land in Tatieh was rented to villagers for cultivation, but belonged to agnatic groups outside the community. As for cross-kin associations claiming village shareholders in 1935, 24 out of 31 in 1935 owned land in Tatieh, the total area being 28 hectares, or about 13 percent of all village farmland. Thus, only 30 percent of all the privae farmland in Tatieh was available to tenants by virtue of their membership in either corporate lineages or cross-kin associations. Since most farmers tenanted land within the village boundaries, it is obvious that cross-kin associations provided nearly as much access to land as did lineages, and that both constituted secondary land sources.

It is important to point out, furthermore, that lineage land was not exclusively rented to holders of shares in the groups concerned. There is reason to believe that a reluctance to rent estate lands to share holders is not uniquely characteristic of Tatieh (cf. Potter 1970: 128). Unlike the lineages described by Freedman, those based in Tatieh did not enjoy the "centripetal force" associated with stratified structures and large landholdings. They provided small periodic distributions, but they offered little in the way of subsidies for education and nothing at all for welfare or litigation.

Although the holdings of lineages and cross-kin associations in Tatieh were small in absolute terms, and although they constituted a secondary source of land through tenancy, the proportion of available land that villagers invested in them suggests that they were considered of some importance. Land data for 1935 suggest that villagers may not have been in a position to sink much more land into either agnatic or associative corporations by that time (see Table 16). Out of 126 hectares of village land owned by "individuals" at least 82 were probably owned by absentee Hokkien landlords, to judge from their holdings on the eve of the Land-to-the-Tiller Program (see Table 9). If this is so, individual villagers together with their lineage and associative corporations owned only 108 hectares of village land, of which corporations already controlled 59 percent (lineages 33 percent and associations 26 percent), or 64 hectares. Since only 44 hectares of land were owned by individual villagers, further corporation building would have been difficult. Indeed, the possibility of further investment in lineage estates by Tatieh villagers might have been better had the 28 hectares of land given to cross-kin associations not been so invested.

CHUNGSHE

At the time of my study in Chungshe, the distribution of family forms was very like that of Tatieh. The vast majority of house-

TABLE 18

Population and Number of Households in Tatieh and Chungshe, 1920–68

Village and category	1920	1935	Percent change since 1920	1964 (Tatieh) / 1968 (Chungshe)	Percent change since 1935
Tatieh					
Households	148	189	27.7%	265	40.2%
Population	809	1,051	29.9	1,602	52.4
Chungshe					
Households	78	87	11.5	194	122.9
Population	364	565	55.2	1,115	97.3

SOURCES: Figures for 1920 and 1935 are based on the Japanese censuses for those years. Those for 1964 and 1968 are based on my own censuses and apply to units comparable to those of 1920 and 1935.

holds consisted of stem or nuclear families, and the median household size was 6.0 persons. In both communities joint families were relatively rare. The Japanese household registers for Chungshe indicate that before 1930 most families with two or more adult sons achieved joint form before dividing.[15] As Table 18 indicates, the number of households in Chungshe rose very gradually between 1920 and 1935, and much more rapidly between 1935 and 1968. The pattern for Tatieh was strikingly different.

Family form and family division. As the table shows, both the number of households and the total resident population have increased more dramatically in Chungshe since the 1930's. The dif-

---

[15] Great care must be exercised in using the household registers to determine family form. One difficulty is that migration is inadequately recorded. The registers are better in this regard for the Japanese period, when most movement was from one village to another and the registrars were police officers familiar with the local scene, than for more recent times, when movement has tended to be toward the large cities. Another difficulty is deliberate deception: both during the Japanese period and after 1945 there were various motives for either registering fictional family divisions or suppressing actual ones. Still more important, family (*chia*) and household (*hu*) are usually but not invariably coordinate. It is possible for a family to consist of several residentially discrete units (*hu*), all of which share a common estate. So long as brothers have not partitioned their family estate, they continue to be members of the same *chia* even if they live in different *hu* (cf. Cohen 1967, 1968). My censuses in Tatieh and Chungshe reveal errors with respect to family form in the contemporary household registers of both villages.

TABLE 19

Family Size in Tatieh and Chungshe, 1946–68

Number of persons per family	Tatieh		Chungshe	
	1946	1964	1946	1968
1	6	7	3	3
2	9	9	9	10
3	24	27	11	10
4	24	26	11	26
5	27	36	15	39
6	35	58	15	41
7	33	39	12	28
8	17	24	8	20
9	11	20	9	9
10	12	4	6	3
11	4	2	4	2
12	0	6	1	1
13	2	1	2	0
14	2	2	1	0
15 and over[a]	2	3	2	1
TOTAL	208	264	109	193
Mean	6.0	6.1	6.3	5.8
Median	6.0	6.0	6.0	6.0
% 7 or more	39.9%	38.3%	41.3%	33.2%

SOURCE: Household registers.

[a] For Tatieh: in 1946, one family of 15, one of 18; in 1964, one of 15, two of 16. For Chungshe: in 1946, one family of 18, one of 26; in 1968, one of 16.

ferential rate of population growth has been mainly the result of a higher birth rate in Chungshe, as Table 11 suggests. In-migration was evidently not an important factor; Chungshe villagers recall only twelve families having moved into the village since 1900. More interestingly, Tables 19 and 20 show a significant reduction in the number of joint families and large families (i.e. those containing seven or more persons) in Chungshe from 1946 to 1968. No significant change in either respect took place in Tatieh. Although 1946 provides our earliest profile of family form and size,[16] it can be inferred that the proportion of joint and large

[16] Because my copies of the household register for Tatieh prior to 1946 are incomplete, I am unable to compare the villages prior to that year. Concerning size of household prior to 1930, no reliable statement can be made on the basis of census materials alone. Since the distribution of family forms cannot be precisely determined, a simple arithmetic mean obtained by dividing total resident population by number of households would be skewed (and differently in both villages) by the presence of very large or very small households.

TABLE 20
Family Form in Tatieh and Chungshe, 1946–68

Family form	Tatieh				Chungshe			
	1946		1964		1946		1968	
	Number	Percent	Number	Percent	Number	Percent	Number	Percent
Joint	10	4.8%	13	4.9%	10	9.2%	3	1.6%
Stem	80	38.5	94	35.6	43	39.4	51	26.4
Nuclear	110	52.9	147	55.7	53	48.6	135	69.9
Other	8	3.8	10	3.8	3	2.8	4	2.1
TOTAL	208	100.0%	264[a]	100.0%	109	100.0%	193	100.0%

SOURCE: Household registers and my own censuses.

[a] One household consisting of residents of the village temple is excluded from these calculations, since the members are in no way related.

families in Chungshe was even greater in 1930, as suggested in my earlier discussion (pp. 48–55).

In comparing changes in family form in Tatieh and Chungshe, no special significance can seemingly be attributed to ethnic differences except for the fact that Hokkien women, unlike their Hakka counterparts, did not work in the fields. In particular, there is no reason to suspect that the Hakka *as an ethnic group* are any more or less prone to form and maintain joint families than Hokkien speakers. Chungshe started out with proportionately more joint families than Tatieh and ended up with fewer; such a change cannot be explained in purely ethnic terms. In Tatieh, joint families of this sort have constituted about 5 percent of all families. But according to Cohen, joint families in Yen-liao (also south Taiwan Hakka) constituted about 32 percent (1967: 639), whereas in Hsin Hsing, a Hokkien village, they constituted, as in Tatieh, only 5 percent (Gallin 1966: 138). Again no purely ethnic explanation makes sense.

Marriage and affinal relations. In Chungshe, as in Tatieh, consideration is given to the instrumental potential of prospective affines, and choices are made with a view to broadening the range of affinal ties. Marital restrictions similar to those in Tatieh are also customary.[17] Unlike the inhabitants of Tatieh, however, Chungshe villagers prefer to select spouses from outside the com-

---

[17] Marriage with first cousins is uncommon. Marriage with a patrilateral parallel cousin is considered particularly undesirable, marriage with a patri-

munity. Marrying within the village, they say, is asking for trouble. If contact between affines is allowed to become too frequent or informal, good relations are likely to deteriorate; and when arguments arise within the family, a wife can all too easily run home to her parents. According to a popular saying, "If affinals live close by, eyes will always be red; if they live far apart, each side will kill a chicken in celebration when they meet." To be sure, arguments are made in favor of marriage within the community. For one thing, such marriages can facilitate mutual help: in the local saying, "While relatives through the penis may have their differences, relatives through the vagina tend to get on smoothly." But the consensus is that the disadvantages of such a marriage far outweigh any advantages.

As we have seen, 48 percent of all brides and the same percentage of grooms taken in marriage by Tatieh villagers were village residents. The percentages for Chungshe were only 21 and 20 percent, respectively. In behavioral terms, then, Chungshe conforms more closely to the model exogamous Chinese community. Consistent with their greater emphasis upon patrilineality, Chungshe villagers more commonly marry in such a way as to ensure a physical separation between affinally related families.

Ceremonial behavior. There are a number of corresponding differences in the handling of family-sponsored ritual activities. We have noted a tendency in Tatieh to play down distinctions between agnates, affines, and friends, to make weddings, funerals, and birthdays occasions for the reaffirmation of ties between non-kin as well as between kin. There are also occasions in Chungshe for reinforcing bonds of affinality and friendship, thanks in part to the completion of the Chianan irrigation system in 1930, which increased

---

lateral cross-cousin somewhat less so. According to a local saying, "A buffalo that returns to the stall does not bear young," and the return of a girl to her mother's agnates in marriage would constitute such a "return to the stall." I know of only one marriage of this sort in Chungshe. As in Tatieh, marriage with a matrilateral parallel cousin is tolerated; so also, though less so, is marriage with a matrilateral cross-cousin. Marriages of the latter type are sometimes justified by the maxim "Add affines upon affines," or reinforce an affinal tie with another affinal tie; but it is still preferable to marry someone to whom one is not related at all.

the need for cooperation across agnatic lines, and to the Land Reform Program, which reduced economic differences between families. Nevertheless, as we shall see, ritually expressed lines between agnates, affines, and friends are still more sharply drawn in Chungshe than in Tatieh.

When a Tatieh villager attains his 61st birthday, and on each tenth anniversary thereafter, his family normally holds an elaborate celebration in his honor. Many friends and relatives through marriage are invited to enjoy the feast that marks the high point of this celebration, and many families cooperate to prepare it. On the analogous occasions in Chungshe, by contrast, the elderly celebrant and his descendants simply worship in the ancestral hall and take lunch together. Birthdays are simple affairs that essentially involve close agnates. The same is true of celebrations marking the birth of a son in Chungshe. On the day before celebrating the "full month" after birth in Tatieh, a father visits his wife's natal home to worship her ancestors. No comparable blending of sacrificial obligations is found in Chungshe, and the full-month feast itself is a relatively simple affair. It does not require extensive cooperation to prepare, and it is essentially intended for the enjoyment of close agnates and a few relatives by marriage.

In weddings the differences between Tatieh and Chungshe are even more apparent. In Tatieh, as we have seen, the groom presents sacrifices to his father's mother's ancestors and those of his own mother. In Chungshe, the groom's obligations are more clearly confined to his own patrilineal ancestors, whose tablets are located in a series of compound halls. In worshiping them, a groom retraces the history of his agnatic group. The building of new compounds and ancestral halls to accommodate an increasing number of agnates does not terminate a person's ceremonial obligations as it does in Tatieh, and a groom does not limit his attention to the more immediate patrilineal ancestors with tablets located in his own compound hall. Unlike his Tatieh counterpart, moreover, the Chungshe groom does not carry sacrifices to the village temple. Instead, gods are borrowed from the temple and brought to his compound hall.

Another difference is that in Chungshe very few of the bride's friends and relatives partake of the feast provided in the groom's home. On one occasion I observed, a groom provided six tables to seat 42 guests, only two of whom were relatives of the bride. Apart from a few friends, the other guests were either agnates of the groom and their spouses or matrilateral relatives. Similarly, on the day after the wedding, when the bride's family provides a feast, very few of the groom's friends and relatives are present. In one instance where thirteen tables were provided to feast 87 people, only four guests were relatives of the groom. The rest were agnates of the bride and their wives, relatives through marriage, or friends. At all weddings, agnates and their spouses constitute the majority of guests.

Still another difference is in the way labor needs for ceremonies are met. In Tatieh, as we have seen, large feasts such as those for weddings and funerals are normally prepared and served by a mixed group of related and unrelated villagers. In Chungshe, such feasts are usually prepared by hired caterers, assisted by close agnates and a few relatives through marriage. There is no parallel in Chungshe to the teams of friends and neighbors in Tatieh that help out at ceremonials. Nor is there anything in Chungshe comparable to Tatieh's father-mother associations. At a funeral the descendants carry the major burden of labor, although they get some help—especially on the burial day—from agnates, relatives through marriage, and a few close neighbors (often themselves agnates), as well as from the professional caterers. That funeral associations were found in Tatieh but not in Chungshe is entirely consistent with the general emphasis in Tatieh on cooperation between families. In particular, this difference cannot be explained in terms of economic differences between the two villages: better off villagers in Tatieh are as quick to rely on funeral associations as the poor, and poor villagers in Chungshe as quick to hire caterers as the better off.

Family perpetuation. Adoption in Chungshe, as in Tatieh, is not uncommon; but the preference for sons of close agnates is acted upon somewhat more frequently. During my stay in Chungshe I found twelve adopted sons and thirteen adopted daughters. Eight of the sons had been obtained from close agnates; none of the daughters had been so acquired. I also discovered several cases of what might be called maid adoption or, more accurately, maid purchase. No arrangements of this sort came to my attention in Tatieh. Only wealthy families can afford to purchase a maid to perform the more unpleasant household tasks. Arrangements of this sort are rare in Chungshe today, but they were apparently quite common during the Japanese period. A number of wealthy villagers (all descendants of Lai Yüan) have owned maids, and a few have owned several at the same time.

Uxorilocal marriages, another rarity in Tatieh, were once common in Chungshe. Data from the household registers show a decline in the number of such marriages over the years, but during each of the periods covered there were more *ju-chui* (i.e. uxorilocal husbands) than male adoptions. In many cases, especially prior to 1930, *ju-chui* entered families that had already provided an heir. In a number of instances their entry into a family resulted in joint form. In still other cases, they were brought into families by marriage with a widow. Two points are worth making here. First, whereas uxorilocal marriages were always rare in Tatieh, they were common in Chungshe until 1930 and thereafter became more infrequent. Second, whereas such marriages mainly provided an alternative mechanism for family perpetuation in Tatieh, many that took place in Chungshe could not have been so motivated, since they involved girls whose brothers had already fathered sons. These facts taken together suggest that uxorilocal marriages may have served an additional purpose in Chungshe— they may have satisfied a need for adult male labor, a need linked to Chungshe's dependence on rainfall. Indeed, in most cases known to me in Chungshe, *ju-chui* were called into families deficient in male labor.

Recent trends. In Chungshe as in Tatieh, the young are growing more independent and developing new attitudes toward marriage and family life. In Chungshe, too, there is increasing off-farm employment and out-migration; pressures to this end are both

more recent and more compelling than in Tatieh. As recently as
the 1930's, Chungshe probably still enjoyed comparatively abundant land resources. Somewhere between 1935 and 1968, however,
the situation changed. Within this period of 33 years the number
of households in Chungshe more than doubled, and the mean
holding dropped from 2.5 to 1.4 hectares. The change in Tatieh
was much less: from 1.2 hectares in 1935 to .8 hectare in 1964.
The more rapid decline in average holding size in Chungshe is
also reflected in data presented in Tables 2, 3, 6, and 7. The total
area cultivated by Tatieh villagers dropped slightly from 1952 to
1964, and the median holding size per household declined by 17.2
percent during the same period. By contrast, whereas the total
cultivated area in Chungshe actually increased from 1953 to 1968,
the median holding size per household declined by 37.8 percent,
more than twice the rate of decline in Tatieh. Chungshe's population has been slow in adjusting to these new restraints (witness
the high birthrate since 1947), and out-migration has accordingly
been considerable. Eighty-nine former villagers (i.e. 8 percent of
the village resident population) are living and working outside
the community. They are drawn from 51 households (i.e. from
26 percent of all village households). According to household
interviews, 93 percent of these out-migrants left home after 1946,
and 62 percent left after 1961.

Agnatic kinship beyond the family. Like their counterparts in
Tatieh, Chungshe villagers recognize agnatic groupings beyond
the level of divided brothers. As we shall see, however, the functional importance of these corporate descent groups within the
community is notably greater than in Tatieh.

From government records and interviews we know that in 1968
Chungshe villagers belonged to ten corporate descent groups, owning a total of 20.3 hectares of land. Despite Chungshe's smaller
population, then, it harbored twice as many descent groups as
Tatieh, and these groups owned nearly six times as much land as
their Tatieh counterparts. In neither community were lineage
estates significantly affected by the Land-to-the-Tiller Program in
1953; indeed, in Chungshe there had been no great change since

1935, when twelve descent groups owned some 23 hectares. At that time Tatieh people belonged to more lineage corporations and the total area owned was greater (see Table 17), but typically these corporations were not localized and did not have their headquarters in the community; their major function was to link communities rather than to highlight distinctions within them. Lineages to which Chungshe villagers belonged, by contrast, were strictly confined to the community. Although a few families with access to lineage properties now live in other places, they were not dispersed when these trusts were created. As we shall see, moreover, the major function of Chungshe's descent groups was not to link communities or agnatic groups within communities, but rather to distinguish among them.

Nine of Chungshe's ten ancestral estates represent branches of a single lineage. This descent group, entrenched in the village "head," has economically and politically dominated the community from its founding. It is also the most internally complex lineage in the village, consisting of corporate branches within corporate branches. More inclusive agnatic corporations in Chungshe are invariably older than less inclusive ones—indicating a development within the maximal descent group that corresponds to the segmentary process described at length by Freedman (1958). This nesting pattern reflects the unequal accumulation of wealth within the maximal descent group as well as a long history of internal squabbling. The establishment of an estate in the name of a particular ancestor presupposes the ability to set land aside as common property. That one ancestor's progeny are sufficiently well off to do this is no guarantee that his brother's descendants will be comparably well off.

Precise genealogical position is a critical determinant of privileges with respect to most ancestral estates in Chungshe. The sons of any ancestor are said to constitute the *fang* of that ancestor. Where an ancestor has become the focus of a corporate estate or trust, his progeny align themselves in terms of fang, with each fang as a group enjoying equal access to the ancestral estate. The sons in the next generation similarly align themselves in terms of

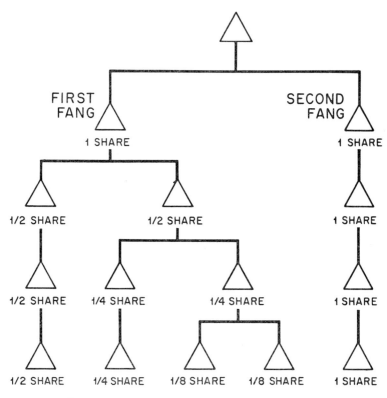

Fig. 6. The development of differential shareholding
in a corporate lineage

less inclusive fang units, each one of which enjoys equal access to
that portion of the total ancestral estate to which their focal ancestor was entitled. As generations succeed each other, then, access to the ancestral properties can become unevenly distributed
among the progeny of the first ancestor. Figure 6 illustrates the
working of this principle. The privileges and responsibilities associated with management of an ancestral trust in Chungshe usually
rotate on the basis of fang, and some portion of the corporation
earnings is normally distributed annually on a share basis. Genealogical position therefore determines both the portion of distributed profit a descendant can expect to receive and how often
he must assume managerial responsibility.

In 1968, the Lai trusts owned between them all but .4 hectare of the total 20.3 hectares belonging to descent groups in the community. Figure 7 indicates the various trusts endowed by the progeny of Lai Yüan, the ancestor chosen to serve as branch focus in each case, and the dates of establishment and dissolution (where applicable). The Lai Yüan estate, established in the name of the first settler, is the oldest extant ancestral trust in Chungshe. Theoretically, all descendants of Lai Yüan are entitled to some share in the profits of this estate, which currently consists of 1.7 hectares of land located in neighboring Liuying township. As is true of lands belonging to all descent groups in Chungshe, these lands may be rented to anyone—agnates or nonagnates, villagers or nonvillagers. Rents provide dividends proportional to shares held, and are also used to offset the costs of periodic sacrifices to the first ancestor and his wife. Worship and sacrifices are provided for the ancestral couple by the descendants of their five fang in accordance with a five-year rotation schedule. The progeny of one fang ancestor now live in the nearby community of Hsiaying but participate in the rotation nonetheless. Each fang maintains the couple's ancestral tablets in its own hall for one year. Not all descent groups, or all fang within descent groups, offer sacrifices on the same occasions, but in all corporations in which responsibilities rotate according to fang only representatives of the host fang need be present when sacrifices are offered. These rites no longer serve as the occasion for a gathering of the descent group.

The profits derived from the Yai Yüan estate were once used to underwrite two lineage feasts every year, given by the fang with the ancestral tablets that year. Only three or four tables, each seating eight persons, were actually required for a lineage feast, since in practice only the eldest surviving members of the various fang attended these banquets, where they represented all younger and lower-generation members of their respective branches. All such banquets in Chungshe were discontinued during the war years and have not been resumed. One reason was that Japanese authorities took pains to discourage them. More important was a deterioration in the relationships between many important and influential members of these descent groups. For many years they

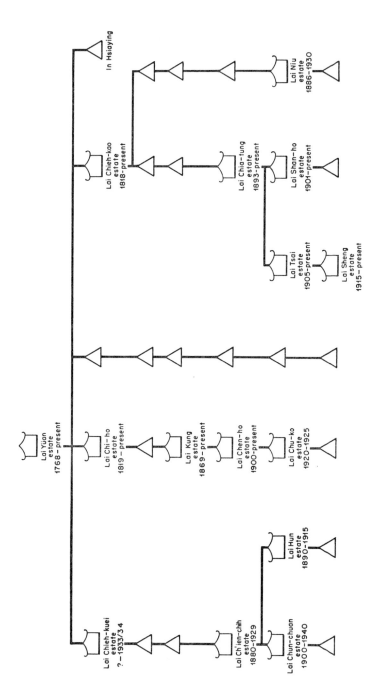

Fig. 7. Ancestral estates of the Lai Yüan lineage, Chungshe village

had been squabbling among themselves over a variety of issues (land, inheritance, adoptions, defense). Relations between Lai Yin-te and her father's agnatic cousin, Lai T'iao-hsing (both powerful and wealthy figures in the community), had so deteriorated, for example, that when Yin-te's turn came to provide the annual feasts T'iao-hsing failed to appear.[18] Because he refused to attend, his sons, brother, and brother's sons also refused. After the arrival of the Japanese, many such rifts developed and solidarity across the various fang ultimately disappeared.

In former times, most of Lai Yüan's progeny lived in two large, fortified adjacent compounds in the village "head." Members of Lai Yüan's fifth fang occupied a third compound close by. There were five ancestral halls, each reserved for the descendants of one of Lai Yüan's fang, and the tablets of the lineage ancestor and his wife were shifted annually from one to the other. On special occasions, sacrifices were required before the tablets of immediate ancestors housed in one's fang hall as well as before the tablets of Lai Yüan and his wife. There was thus a ritually expressed hierarchy of halls within the descent group for which we find no parallel in Tatieh. This nesting pattern was gradually elaborated as new halls and corporate branches were established within the community. To this day, as we have seen, marriage ritual often requires that sacrifices be carried to ancestors located in several halls.

Although shares in the Lai ancestral trusts are theoretically allocated on a purely genealogical basis, being equally divided among sons at each generation level, their actual distribution is somewhat different. Within the descent group shares may be bought or sold, given or received as gift, or acquired by default. From time to time there are conflicts over shares with little absolute value, often with an eye to more basic conflicts involving significant rewards. For example, two kinsmen may compete for a particular share because its possession would add legitimacy to a claim on someone's personal property. By way of illustration, let us examine one such struggle.

[18] Lai Yin-te married a *ju-chui* and provided lineage feasts in her father's name.

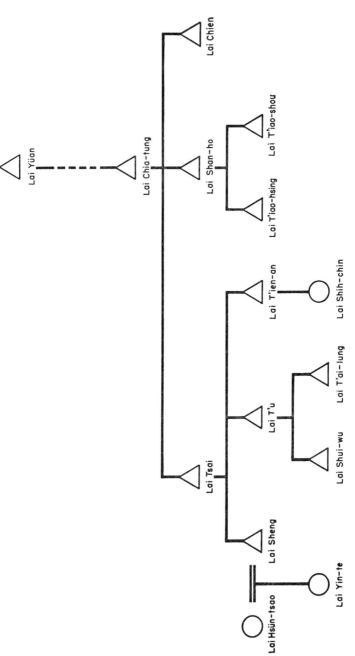

Fig. 8. Genealogical background for descent group conflicts (abbreviated)

Around 1915, Lai Hsün-tsao finally agreed to adopt Lai T'ai-lung, the son of her husband's brother Lai T'u (see Fig. 8). For years her late husband, Lai Sheng, had rejected Lai T'u's plea that he adopt this boy, since he hoped to the last to have a son of his own. When it became clear that Sheng was dying, T'u and his cousin Lai T'iao-hsing became anxious that T'ai-lung be recorded as Sheng's son before the registration of death, since otherwise it would be difficult to register the boy as Sheng's adopted son. The household registers at that time were in the hands of local police authorities. When Lai T'u and Lai T'iao-hsing attempted to register the adoption, the local police official, a personal friend of Lai Sheng, suspected mischief. He stalled action on the adoption and sent word to Lai Hsün-tsao that some of her husband's agnates were attempting to record an adoption that could enable them to gain control over her husband's property. "Even if these men beat you," he reportedly advised her, "and no matter what I may say to you in the government office, you must refuse to consent to this adoption." Lai Hsün-tsao, by then a widow, immediately went to the police station, where she created a row. For the time being, therefore, the adoption was postponed.

After considerable negotiation, Lai Hsün-tsao finally agreed to register Lai T'ai-lung as her own adopted son. It is important to note that since he was adopted to her rather than to her late husband, T'ai-lung was not legally entitled to inherit Lai Sheng's personal property. As part of the adoption agreement, however, the widow consented to confer upon her adoptive son, in the form of a "gift," two hectares of land out of her husband's private estate of twenty hectares. Since T'ai-lung was her adopted son, furthermore, he was not entitled to inherit Lai Sheng's shares in various descent group estates. By registering the adoption in this way, then, Lai Hsün-tsao managed to ensure that no convincing claim could be made by T'ai-lung and that her late husband's property would be passed to her two daughters (one of whom subsequently married a ju-chui), through whom she was able to maintain her control over her husband's estate as long as she lived.

Since Lai T'ai-lung had not in fact been adopted by Lai Sheng, or played the role of son at his uncle's funeral, his only chance of establishing a claim to his uncle's estate was to show that he had inherited his uncle's shares in various ancestral estates. A struggle accordingly emerged over these shares between Lai T'ai-lung and Lai Hsün-tsao, in which Lai Sheng's property was the only significant consideration. Although he ultimately lost this struggle, T'ai-lung's chances of winning it were by no means negligible, thanks to the common belief in Chungshe that special pains should be taken to avoid alienation of shares in ancestral trusts to persons other than agnates. Alienation is clearly more likely where the inheritor is a woman. This story illustrates one way in which cleavages can emerge or be perpetuated within a descent group, particularly when no outside threat encourages suppression of fissive tendencies. In the next chapter, I will discuss other incidents that served to divide the descendants of Lai Yüan.

FOUR

Village Integration

TATIEH IS a highly integrated community; villagers take an active interest in its affairs, and there is a strong feeling of solidarity. Chungshe is very different; a variety of rifts and antagonisms detract from its ability to function as a village in its own interests.

Tatieh's village headmen, drawn from a number of descent groups, have for many years played a major role in mediation. In Chungshe, by contrast, headmen were important as mediators only before 1945, when they were drawn exclusively from the dominant descent group. Since Restoration (1945) and Land Reform (1953), headmen have come from other descent groups, and their importance as mediators has declined.

Social relations in both communities cross boundaries of neighborhood and kinship, but they do so to a lesser extent in Chungshe. In Tatieh a number of corporate sodalities, or cross-kin associations, have served to promote interfamilial cooperation and village unity. The few associations of this sort in Chungshe have tended to reflect, and occasionally to reinforce, social and economic divisions within the community.

For certain ceremonial purposes—notably annual festivals—a Chinese village functions as a unit, with activities organized at the community level and centering on the village temple. Such ceremonies provide an occasion for the expression of community solidarity in both Tatieh and Chungshe, but the differences between the two villages are far more striking than the similarities.

TATIEH

The formal administrative structure of all Taiwanese villages provides for a *ts'un-chang*, or village headman, elected by ballot for a term of four years; a *ts'un kan-shih*, or village secretary, appointed by the Township Office; and a village council consisting of informally elected *lin-chang*, or neighborhood chiefs.[1] The headman is the official community representative at the township level; at the same time, he represents higher-level governments to his constituents in the village. His functions include coordinating community activities, handling village finances, presiding over village meetings and ceremonies, and resolving conflicts. He is also ex-officio chairman of the village council.

Being village headman or a neighborhood chief in Tatieh is a demanding job, but confers only limited prestige and authority. The headman makes no important decisions on behalf of the community without the explicit approval of the village council or household heads. His authority is restricted by public opinion, and his activities are subject to public review and criticism. Tatieh's headman came under attack on several occasions during my stay. In one instance he was reprimanded at a meeting of the village council for maintaining community records in a haphazard manner; criticism was initiated by a neighborhood chief of different surname, but others present, some agnatically related to the headman, joined in.

Major policy decisions affecting Tatieh are most often made during village meetings, convened roughly every two months,

[1] Tatieh consists of seventeen *lin*, or administrative "neighborhoods," of which thirteen form the village proper. Two others, located about 1.2 kilometers to the north, have been an administrative part of Tatieh for 50 years. In 1911, when a flood in nearby Changlung resulted in ruin for many families, seven families (all named Ch'en but apparently unrelated to Ch'en families already residing in Tatieh) resettled in this area, where they cultivated land controlled by the sugar refinery. Fifteen of the 36 households now living in these two neighborhoods are descendants of these original seven families; the other 21 are more recent arrivals of various surnames. About 31 families live in another two neighborhoods, located less than a kilometer south of the village. Many of them are Hsinchu Hakka who emigrated from the north of Taiwan some 30 years ago.

which are attended by an adult male representative from each household. Because being a headman or neighborhood chief does not constitute an effective stepping-stone to personal profit or higher political office, these positions normally do not attract better educated, politically ambitious, or wealthier villagers. In my experience, headmen and neighborhood chiefs tend to be relatively uneducated men who enjoy a reputation for fairness, sound judgment, and public spirit.

Kinship and village administration. Tatieh's present headman, like most of his recent predecessors, has one of the three most common surnames in the village, though his more specific affiliation is with a small group of families all of whom trace descent from a common ancestor. No regularities are apparent with regard to alternation among these groups. Neighborhood chiefs sometimes have a surname that is poorly represented in the neighborhood they represent. In mixed neighborhoods, they are not consciously chosen from any particular surname group, and their selection does not involve a pattern of rotation among the various surnames represented. Only where families of a given surname constitute a distinct majority do neighborhood chiefs repeatedly come from a particular surname group, and here the same pattern might be expected by random selection.

If agnatic affiliation plays little role in the selection of village officials, it plays even less part in determining the way village administration is conducted. Whenever activities must be organized at the community level, it is invariably households and not agnatic groups that constitute the units to be articulated. A few examples will illustrate this point.

For each male between 18 and 50 (excluding students and soldiers), a household is required to donate ten days of public labor or a monetary equivalent every year. The use to which this labor will be put is decided at the township level, but mobilization, organization, and administration of work details are arranged at the village level. Compulsory labor is assigned to households on the basis of their neighborhood distribution. So long as tasks assigned are intended to improve conditions within the village, little resistance is encountered. In fact, competition between the various villages of the township (e.g. in road building) is taken seriously. At one village council meeting, it was suggested that a portion of road to be built by common labor be set aside for villagers who had failed to meet their obligations the previous year, thus exposing these delinquents as a warning to others. Some neighborhood chiefs objected that a few stubborn men doing a poor job could put the whole community at a disadvantage in the township competition, and the portion to be built by the delinquents was accordingly shortened.

Night watches are also assigned on a household basis rather than an agnatic basis. From the middle of the twelfth month to the middle of the first month, a community night watch is set up to guard against thieves and fire. Fires are frequent because this is the high point of the dry season, thievery because this is the time when household finances are most strained, "when the yellow rice of the last crop does not meet the green rice of the next." Six men aged 18 to 50, provided by households on a rotational basis, take turns on watch.

Public sanitation is another general responsibility. Before all major festivals, and before visits by important personages, the headman usually calls for a general cleanup. Each household cleans the area around its own dwelling, and villagers whose homes face the street clean the roadway directly in front of their dwellings. Households are also periodically called on to contribute labor or money for cleaning and repairing public drainage systems.

The way conflicts are resolved provides another indication of the way community integration is achieved. Disputes between households are first thrashed out between the heads of the households involved. If no solution is reached, the case is usually brought to the headman for arbitration. He hears both sides, calls whatever witnesses may be necessary, and suggests a compromise only where the disputants are unable to effect a satisfactory solution themselves. He has no power to enforce his decision. Should his mediation fail, however, the only recourse would be to an arbitration committee at the township level or to a court of law.

Conflicts that actually reach this stage are rare. During my stay in Tatieh, a variety of disputes were brought to the headman for arbitration, some involving persons of the same surname, others concerned with persons of different surname. The parties involved were individuals, not representatives of agnatic groups. The head-man himself might or might not have agnatic ties with one of the disputants.

Since late Ch'ing times there have been changes affecting village administrative structure. According to older informants, consid-erable authority once resided with the more prestigious members of various agnatic groups. In pre-Japanese times, disputes between agnatically related families were resolved by the older and wealth-ier members of the group concerned, and disputes between fami-lies not agnatically related were settled by respected personages of both groups. More general conflicts between surname groups were commonly settled by a consensus of influential men of various sur-names. Such men in those years did not simply play the role of moderators by invitation. When they determined that a conflict was injurious to the community, they would summon the parties concerned to a convenient place, hear both sides, and impose a settlement.

In 1898, the Japanese instituted the *pao-chia* system of collec-tive responsibility on Taiwan in an effort to ensure social sta-bility and rural control with a minimum of police interference. Ideally, the plan called for the grouping of ten households to form a *chia*, under a *chia-chang*, or *chia* chief; ten *chia* consti-tuted a *pao*, which was placed under the authority of a *pao-cheng*, or *pao* chief. The *chia* and *pao* in Japanese times roughly corre-sponded to what are now termed neighborhood and village. It was Japanese policy to select as *chia* and *pao* chiefs important members of the larger surname groups in a community. Accord-ing to older villagers (including a former *pao* chief), Japanese pol-icy created a single overriding authority in Tatieh where before there had been none. The *pao* chief's authority was bolstered by the local police and by a specially created "local defense corps" (*chuang-ting t'uan*). He had the right to summon offenders or dis-putants to his office and the authority to enforce his decisions.

As noted earlier, the retrocession of Taiwan to Chinese administration in 1945 brought marked changes. Education was extended, physical mobility increased, and the land reform diminished economic differences between families. As Tatieh increasingly became part of a larger society, power and influence shifted somewhat from the old and wealthy to the young and educated, resulting in a diffusion of power and influence within the community. Since Ch'ing times, then, there has been a shift in the locus of community authority and leadership from influential personages representing various agnatic groups to the office of *pao* chief, then to the heads of individual households, and finally to a variety of individual villagers. At no point in Tatieh's history did a single descent group manage to dominate the village politically, economically, or socially.

The community as an economic unit. The economics of community action in Tatieh tell the same story. Public sacrifices, feasts, puppet shows, bands, buses, temple repairs, etc., are costly. So is electricity for the street lights on Tatieh's main street. These public expenditures are partially provided for by the village treasury, which derives its income from a number of sources. Each male villager is assessed roughly NT$2.5 a year in *ting-ch'ien*, or "male money," which is collected by neighborhood chiefs just before New Year. Additional assessments are periodically made for unusual public expenses. Another source of some NT$3,500 a year is colloquially referred to as *ya-ch'ang ch'ien*, or "duck-field money," fees paid by the highest bidder among local duck raisers for the privilege of allowing ducks to feed on insects in all fields within the village boundaries at certain points in the agricultural cycle. The major single source of income to the village treasury is the "Make Prosperous Limited Shares Corporation," whose substantial contributions to meet particular village expenses are formally requested by the village council and granted on approval of the corporation's board of directors. Records of the "Make Prosperous Corporation" indicate that NT$5,000 is set aside each year for village use.

The corporation's history dates from the late Ch'ing, when villagers in Nanan and Tatieh helped to finance dike construction and reforestation projects designed to reduce flooding in the area (see Chung, n.d.). Early in the Japanese period, a few wealthy Nanan villagers somehow managed to have the jointly financed forest covertly registered in their own names. When Tatieh's villagers discovered what had been done, they held a meeting and designated six prosperous men of various surnames to take the case to court. Litigation costs were paid by subscription among village households, with the understanding that, should the case be won, a corporation would be formed in which each contribution of five Japanese *yen* would be worth one share.

Tatieh was ultimately awarded 17 out of the 40 hectares involved. The land was temporarily registered in the names of four of the six litigants, and later the holdings were officially incorporated as the "Make Prosperous Limited Shares Corporation." The four initial trustees were granted 50 shares each for their services, all contributors were given shares as previously agreed, and additional shares were made available for sale to any villager who had been a resident of Tatieh for six months. There are now 1,650 shares in circulation among 205 households, with nearly every household owning at least one share. Shareholders are paid an annual dividend of about NT$100 per share, and each share is worth about NT$200. The corporation's land assets are estimated to be now worth at least NT$2 million. Sugarcane is grown on some thirteen or fourteen of its seventeen hectares; some of the rest is planted in bananas and cotton.

The corporation's board of directors and board of supervisors are elected by all shareholders once every three years from a slate of candidates drawn from members who possess a specified minimum number of shares. The nature of the enterprise makes nepotism or ethnic exclusiveness all but impossible. Sugarcane is grown for sale to the refinery; bananas, sweet potatoes, and most agricultural by-products are sold to the highest bidder. Although Tatieh villagers are theoretically favored in the employment of field labor, wages are uniform and most workers in fact come from neighboring communities. Contracts for special constructions (e.g.

pumps and wells) are given out only after extensive shopping and pricing. In 1964 one such contract was awarded to a Hokkien builder in Chaochou in preference to a villager related to two members of the board of directors (agnatically to one and affinally to the other). At board meetings, agnatically related members frequently oppose each other on specific issues.

Moreover, the "Make Prosperous Corporation," being virtually coterminous with the community itself, sometimes acts as a unit against outside forces. In the spring of 1962, for example, the corporation applied to the government for permission to plant coconuts and hardwood trees on most of its government-protected "forest preserve." In September, permission was granted to convert the preserve for these specific crops. The forest was cut by December, and in January sugarcane was planted on thirteen or fourteen hectares. When government authorities promptly ordered the sugarcane plowed up, the corporation protested that it had planted sugarcane as an interim measure because its coconut seedlings had not yet arrived from the Philippines. When the seedlings did arrive, the corporation again failed to plant them, and in August 1963 government authorities issued an ultimatum: either the corporation would plant the agreed crops by July 1964 or the government would plant the entire area itself. The headman and various members of the corporation initiated action to achieve a further postponement, while the board of directors hired a well-connected lawyer to investigate the possibility of changing the land's official designation from "forest preserve" to ordinary "dry fields." When I left Tatieh the issue had not yet been resolved.

A similar incident involved a retired soldier, a mainlander colonel, who with his aboriginal wife took up residence on land claimed by the "Make Prosperous Corporation." The land in question was public land, and both parties submitted claims to it through official channels. When the soldier proceeded to violate government regulations by cutting timber on this land, several villagers haled him to court, where he was excused "because of his former service to his country." The court ordered him to plant new trees to replace those he had cut, but he ignored the order.

One morning the headman, who was also at that time manager of the "Make Prosperous Corporation," summoned eight or nine villagers to his office. The corporation had hired several aborigines to prepare the contested area for planting sugarcane, and these villagers were to go along with the headman to forestall any outside interference. As anticipated, the colonel protested vehemently, and local police had to be called in to prevent violence. In the end, the "Make Prosperous Corporation" won its point and planted the contested fields.

Community solidarity and external challenge. Tatieh has long been troubled by ethnic tensions and hostilities. Although overt fighting between Hakka and Hokkien was suppressed by the Japanese and the old antagonisms have softened over time, conflicts still periodically occur. When they do, Tatieh invariably acts as a unit in its own interests.

Relations between Tatieh and the small Hokkien village of Shoufu, two kilometers to the west, have frequently been characterized by violent conflicts over water, grazing rights, crops, and cultivated land. Conflicts between neighboring communities are not rare in China; and as our discussion of the Tatieh-Nanan litigation shows, they do not always reflect ethnic differences. But in the difficulties between Tatieh and Shoufu, ethnic differences have been prominent. In the past, Shoufu and other nearby Hokkien communities frequently joined forces against Tatieh and its Hakka neighbors; and no one that I spoke to in either village could recall any alliance, however temporary, between Shoufu and a Hakka village or between Tatieh and a Hokkien village. Residents of the two communities still view each other with suspicion and disdain. When Tatieh villagers built a pagoda and crematorium near the provincial highway that passes between the two settlements several years ago, many Shoufu people resented this display of prosperity. Shortly thereafter Shoufu suffered a series of misfortunes, which its inhabitants attributed to hungry ghosts turned away from Tatieh by these structures.

A seemingly typical flare-up of the antagonism between Shoufu and Tatieh took place during my stay in Tatieh. Young men and women from both villages periodically work in the fields of the sugar refinery. One day, as I reconstruct the story from fragments provided by residents of both communities, a young lady from Shoufu took to flirting with several young men from Tatieh. For several days she favored them with suggestive remarks. One evening, while some Tatieh boys were passing time at the bus stop near the village turnoff from the provincial highway, the young lady of Shoufu came by with a young man from her village. According to Shoufu villagers, the Tatieh boys made insulting remarks; according to Tatieh villagers, the couple deliberately provoked such remarks. The next two evenings, the girl again passed the bus stop accompanied by a young man from her village. Tatieh people claim that this was a deliberate attempt to incite trouble. On the fourth night several youngsters from Tatieh, while grazing buffalo together near the bus stop, were set upon and beaten by a group of Shoufu boys. When word of the assault reached Tatieh, many villagers urged retaliation. The next night, a group of young men from Tatieh secluded themselves near the bus stop, where in due course they pounced on several young men from Shoufu and beat them up.

Ethnic confrontations of this sort are by no means confined to Tatieh and Shoufu. On another occasion an old man from Nanan, a Hakka, returning at night from Chaochou on his bicycle, took a road to Tatieh that passed through several small Hokkien hamlets and an area of sugarcane fields. As he passed these fields, he was set upon by some twenty Hokkien youths and severely beaten. When word of the incident reached Tatieh and its neighboring Hakka communities, there was great anger and excitement. Tatieh villagers were especially enraged that such a thing should happen on the road to their settlement. The village headman appealed for calm and reason, but the next night a little boy, taking the same route as the old man, was insulted and beaten by a gang of Hokkien youths. Villagers decided that some action was necessary to prevent further outrages. Accompanied by several policemen summoned from Hsinpi, a party of twenty Tatieh youths set out along the road to find the assailants. They were unsuccessful, but went again the next night and took cover in cane fields along the edge of the road. After setting up an ambush for several nights without making contact, they finally abandoned the plan and anger in the village gradually subsided. Several young men suggested that a group be sent to Chaochou to beat up a few Hokkien, but most villagers opposed the suggestion as too likely to lead to a major confrontation.

Community solidarity and internal challenge. These incidents show that Tatieh is more than a collectivity of households or surname groups sharing a common territory. It is more than an administrative entity. Villagers take pride in their community and are capable of acting in concert to protect its integrity. The village is by no means free of factional cleavages or interpersonal antagonisms, but where community interests are concerned such differences, like those of kinship and social status, are usually submerged for the common good. Factionalism rarely involves pitting one agnatic group against another. Indeed, as the following story indicates, loyalty to a friend may well pit agnates against each other.

During the Japanese period, Ch'en Chin-hsiang, a relatively wealthy and highly respected villager, became village headman. His relationship with his agnatic cousin's children, Ch'en Ta-ming and Ch'en Li-tung, was a paternalistic one. After their father died, he had been like a father to them. Ch'en Ta-ming never forgot this and treated the old man with respect, but his brother Li-tung "knew no gratitude" and his relationship with Ch'en Chin-hsiang and his sons became worse over the years. Toward the end of the Japanese period, Ch'en Ta-ming, Ch'en Li-tung, and their brother-in-law, Yeh Ta-chang, managed to accumulate considerable power in the community. Ch'en Ta-ming became head of the "local defense corps" and took advantage of his position to oppress and brutalize his fellow villagers. After the departure of the Japanese in 1945, Ch'en Ta-ming was appointed mayor of the township and Yeh Ta-chang became headman in Tatieh. Villagers, still laboring under fears instilled by the Japanese, allowed themselves to be further bullied by these men. Gradually, however, a new faction emerged to threaten their control over the village.

One of Ch'en Chin-hsiang's sons, Ch'en Hao-jen, had served as a clerk in the Township Office under the Japanese. After 1945 the government sent him to Taipei to be trained as a civil administrator. From Taipei he was sent to Kaohsiung, where he served in a minor bureaucratic post until he resigned and returned to Tatieh. There he became offended by Ch'en Ta-ming's behavior and set about mobilizing his many friends and acquaintances in and around Tatieh to oust Ch'en Ta-ming from office.

He soon discovered that he had insufficient capital to replace Ta-ming himself, nor could he depend on support from his father, who continued to harbor paternalistic feelings toward Ch'en Ta-ming. Hao-jen therefore encouraged another villager, Liu Hua-hsiang, who had just returned from a period of study in Japan, to compete with Ta-ming for the Kuomintang nomination for mayor. Like Hao-jen, Liu was a member of the Kuomintang. He was bright, dignified, pleasant, and relatively well off, but he did not enjoy the contacts available to Hao-jen.

With Liu's consent Hao-jen set out to capture as many Kuomintang nominating votes as he could. Seventeen votes were involved. He spent days calculating ways of soliciting votes, trying to see how each voter might be reached and persuaded through either mutual friends or relatives. Finally, he called a secret strategy meeting to which he invited a number of his friends. As a result of decisions made at this meeting, he acquired twelve out of the seventeen votes, three more than the nine he needed. Two he obtained through the mediation of a friend whom he had recommended for a job, another from a close friend whom he personally persuaded. Still another voter, a woman, was won over by a relative living in another township, who in turn had been persuaded to help by a close friend of Hao-jen. This was a particularly difficult vote to get because the woman owed her employment to Ch'en Ta-ming. Four additional votes were controlled by mainlanders, who were persuaded to vote properly by mutual friends. Liu Hua-hsiang and his cousin themselves controlled two votes. Using such tactics, Hao-jen eventually managed to corner a majority of the nominating votes for his candidate.

When word of Hao-jen's activities reached Ch'en Ta-ming, he

called a kind of "peace meeting" to which he invited Liu Hua-hsiang, Hua-hsiang's cousin Liu Tung-yün (Ta-ming's childhood friend and Hao-jen's best friend), Ch'en Li-tung, Ch'en Hao-jen's elder brother, two mainlanders, and other influential villagers of various surnames. Liu was asked to withdraw from the competition, and Hao-jen's faction was urged to give up its support of his candidacy. Hao-jen's elder brother and his best friend were both encouraged to appeal to him to cease his politicking on behalf of Liu Hua-hsiang. Even Hao-jen's father was subsequently persuaded to apply pressure and urge his son to shift his support to Ch'en Ta-ming. "How can you support Hua-hsiang?" he demanded. "Ta-ming is your kinsman and on that ground alone deserves your support. Hua-hsiang is not even of your surname!" But Hao-jen stood firm, replying among other things that Hua-hsiang was his close friend and therefore deserving of loyalty. "In such a situation," he argued, "village dignity and unity are more important than surname. We shall have neither dignity nor unity if Ta-ming is elected."

A variety of threats and pressures failed to move Hao-jen's faction. Liu was duly nominated, and Hao-jen and his fellows set out to win the general election against three candidates from other communities. Most Tatieh villagers actively supported Liu "in the village interest," including some of Ta-ming's close agnates and colleagues; and in the end they obtained a sufficient number of votes from friends and relatives in neighboring communities to elect Liu as mayor. This was the beginning of a rapid climb to political prominence, during which, according to some of my informants, he turned his back on many of his supporters and fellow villagers. And yet he has continued to enjoy the support of virtually all Tatieh villagers in every election. His success not only gives Tatieh important political leverage but reflects credit on his fellow villagers in a way each feels personally.

Membership in what factions exist in Tatieh does not appear to be primarily determined by agnatic considerations; friendship and other relationships are at least as important. Nor does kinship in any way restrict the choice of friends and acquaintances, as it did, for example, in pre-Communist Nanching (a multilineage village in Kwangtung), where "kinship relations represented the paramount force tying the individual into a tightly knit organization beyond which he contracted few direct and intimate social bonds" (C. K. Yang 1959b: 81). The only real obstacles to the formation of friendship in Tatieh—or for that matter beyond its boundaries—are differences of generation and sex.

Association and community integration. One of Tatieh's hallmarks has always been the impressive number, inclusiveness, and effectiveness of its corporate associations based fundamentally on friendship. As indicated earlier, Tatieh once had many more such associations than it has today. In 1935, to judge from documents and interviews, Tatieh had some 31 corporate associations, not counting funeral societies or grain associations. These associations owned about 17 percent of all cultivated village land, or nearly as much as the 23 percent owned by lineages (see Table 16). In the light of community studies done elsewhere in China, and of my Chungshe data, the number and economic viability of these associations as late as the 1930's would seem most unusual.

Although many associations vanished as a result of Japanese colonial policies and, to a lesser extent, in response to the Nationalist land reform, others still exist and are active in the community. We are already familiar with Tatieh's grain associations and funeral societies, and with the village-wide "Make Prosperous Limited Shares Corporation." Another association of interest is the Yen-shou Hui, or "Advanced Age Society." When the most recent version of this association for men aged 60 and over was organized in 1949, some 34 men, representing a variety of surnames and neighborhoods, paid the required entrance fee of 50 catties of rice. The association's fund, now approximately 5,000 catties, is lent to members at moderate interest. Once a year members meet to worship the Heaven God and enjoy a feast. Deceased members are represented by a survivor at such times. The association's assets pay the cost of all convocations and provide special awards to members on their 71st, 81st, and 91st birthdays. The monetary equivalent of 50 catties of rice is provided the family of

a member immediately upon his death, and dividends are distributed to all members at each annual meeting. Members are
expected to attend each other's family-sponsored weddings, funerals, and birthday celebrations. Despite the society's economic advantages, it was initially established as a social organization. As
with a funeral society, when all original members are dead their
survivors will divide up any of the society's remaining assets and
dissolve it.

In addition to villager-generated associations, there are others
inspired or supported by the government. The Koumintang operates a cell in the community with fifteen unenthusiastic members
of various surnames. Some villagers participate in a local equivalent of our Parent-Teachers Association, and a number of youngsters are active in 4H clubs sponsored by the Farmers Association.
Two women are members of the township's two women's associations. Since societies of all these sorts are found throughout Taiwan, however, they are of less interest to us than the indigenous
associations previously described.

Ritual and community. Most of Tatieh's associations have in
one way or another been linked to religious or ritual objectives.
Some, like the Matsu Association or the Kuanti Society, were associated with particular deities; others, like the funeral societies, are
designed to help villagers fulfill their ritual responsibilities. In
contrast to ancestor worship, however, which unites agnates while
at the same time distinguishing groups of agnates from each other,
Tatieh's religious practices have typically been open to all families in the community, and in many cases have actively furthered
community solidarity.

Tatieh's religious life centers in its main temple and around
several smaller shrines. Villagers take special pride in these structures, which are virtually the only community resources to which
all villagers enjoy equal access. The temple is an imposing edifice,
boasting two towers, a nursery, and a small dormitory for lay devotees. Like all other community shrines, the temple was built and
is maintained on the basis of assigned and voluntary contributions.
Supplementary funds are periodically furnished from the village

treasury and from the profits of the "Make Prosperous Corporation." Temple regulars, mainly older men and women, gather in the temple each morning and evening to worship and socialize. Their common interest in the temple has provided a basis for close friendship and mutual aid. Many more villagers visit the temple on the first and fifteenth of each lunar month to offer incense, and every evening several people go to the temple to consult the gods about personal problems. Divining devices are kept there expressly for this purpose. For complex problems (e.g. for advice on how to cure an illness, where and when to build a new house, or how to induce conception of a son), a villager may invite a village medium to consult the gods on his behalf. A great many village families send children to the temple nursery school.

The most important ceremonial occasions in Tatieh are the New Year, the Making Happiness Festival, the Festival of Graves, the Matsu Festival, and the Festival of Hungry Ghosts. The following summary description of these occasions is intended only to highlight an important characteristic common to them all, namely that they involve considerable coordination and expenditure at the village level.

On the fifteenth day of the twelfth month, villagers offer thanks to the village gods for good fortune bestowed upon them during the year and for an anticipated good year to come. All temple gods are worshiped, and in the evening a public sacrifice is offered to the Heaven God and his host in front of the temple. The public treasury helps pay for this sacrifice and for a band hired for the occasion. Three people officiate over the day's ceremonies: the headman, the main village medium, and a ceremonial organizer known as the *fu-chu*, or "Happiness Master," who is elected by lot from among applicants in a different quadrant of the community each year. A number of interested old men of various surnames also assist. On New Year's Eve, villagers worship their ancestors and the gods that dwell in their homes. The following day, after again worshipping their ancestors, they carry sacrifices to the temple gods.

Tso-fu, or "Making Happiness," follows closely upon New Year.

The various activities involved in the Making Happiness Festival are coordinated by the Happiness Master. On the afternoon of the ninth day of the first month, the Happiness Master, the headman, the chief medium, and a number of other villagers "invite the gods." Accompanied by banners, gongs, a hired band, and a multitude of children, these representatives collect several gods that dwell in various shrines and private homes and carry them to the temple. Women who have given birth to sons during the year are then invited to present their *hsin-ting ping*, or "new-male cakes," in the temple. In the evening, all households provide sacrifices in the temple and a community sacrifice is offered to the Heaven God and his host in the temple plaza.

The next morning, village ceremonial leaders conduct an elaborate sacrificial rite in the temple, and most villagers come to offer incense and worship the gods. At noon, all villagers 60 years of age and over, all women who have given birth to sons during the year, all neighborhood chiefs, the headman, and a miscellany of important outside guests are feasted at community expense. In the afternoon, the new mothers distribute their "new-male cakes," one to every village household except those of other new mothers. With suitable pomp and ceremony, the gods that have been brought to the temple are returned to their respective shrines.

Ch'ing-ming, the Festival of Graves, is celebrated by all families on the same day during the second lunar month. In preparation, villagers visit the cemetery to weed and repair the tombs of their ancestors. Then, at a time stipulated by the headman, every family presents its sacrifices before the ancestral tombs. "In former times" each household is said to have presented a sacrifice before each tomb containing its ancestors, but today households closely related by agnation usually economize by dividing up sacrificial responsibilities. While offerings of food and paper clothing are being presented at the graves, it is as though the entire community had suddenly shifted location; only the aged and infirm remain at home. The cemetery is crowded with villagers milling about and socializing.

Soon after the Festival of Graves, during the third month, comes the village's most important festival, that of the goddess Matsu, the main village deity. Preparations for the festival begin long in advance. The village council convenes several times to work out procedures, and a meeting of all household heads is called to solicit suggestions and opinions. The usual sequence of events is for Matsu and an assemblage of other gods to be carried on an inspection tour of her domain. Her parade through the village is marked by great excitement. Altars bearing sacrifices of food and incense are set up in front of compound gates. Watermelon stalls, slingshot ranges, and cotton candy stalls line the roadside as the procession passes. A puppet show is given to mark the occasion. After the gods have returned to the temple, every household provides a sacrifice in the temple for their enjoyment.

The next morning, the village as a whole performs an elaborate sacrificial rite in the temple. At noon, every household feasts friends and relatives from other communities. Acquaintances are literally dragged off the streets as they pass and urged to eat and drink. No family spares expense or effort on this occasion.

Several days before the Matsu Festival during my stay in Tatieh, the three images of Matsu housed in the temple were transported to Peikang, a town in central Taiwan, by a large delegation of villagers. Peikang is reportedly the earliest center of Matsu worship on the island; it was from the temple there that the fire (i.e. incense) of the goddess was originally taken to Tatieh. The trip to Peikang entailed considerable negotiation, expense, and advance planning: a bus had to be hired and hotel accommodations arranged for two nights. The costs of this trip were borne in part by the "Make Prosperous Corporation" and in part by those villagers who made the pilgrimage.

Finally, there is *chung-yüan chieh*, the Festival of Hungry Ghosts, celebrated on the fifteenth day of the seventh month. People who die accidentally, are murdered, or leave no progeny behind to worship them become hungry ghosts. Such ghosts, being angry and malevolent, must be periodically propitiated, but the need is greatest during the seventh month, when ghosts are released from hell and free to roam the earth.

All village households propitiate hungry ghosts on the same day. On the morning of the fifteenth, villagers worship their ancestors and compound gods. In the afternoon, at a time specified by the headman, they present their sacrifices to the hungry ghosts before the village temple. The headman, accompanied by a number of villagers with ceremonial interests and skills, then goes to the west (main) entrance of the village to invite the wandering ghosts to enter and enjoy the food that has been set out for them in front of the temple. On one occasion I counted sixteen villagers, men of various surnames and from various parts of the village, assisting the headman in the ritual of inviting the ghosts.

Before the ghosts are invited to enter the village, most of the village gods are carried out to the temple plaza to supervise the feast. Sacrificial altars are arranged in a circle around a central offering, which is provided by the community as a unit, and a Buddhist priest is hired to direct a special propitiatory ritual. While the ghosts consume the essence of these offerings, villagers visit and worship at a number of nearby shrines.

In these brief descriptions I have tried to make it clear that the village temple functions as a focal point for much of Tatieh's ceremonial activity, that households frequently act in concert to achieve common ritual objectives, and that their concerted activities are coordinated at the village level rather than in terms of family or lineage.

CHUNGSHE

Chungshe's formal administrative structure is much the same as Tatieh's. There is a headman, a secretary, and a village council consisting of informally elected neighborhood chiefs.[2] There is one other high official in Chungshe who has no counterpart in Tatieh—the village accountant, who draws up the budget for community activities, directs the collection of funds, and supervises all village expenditures. In Tatieh these functions are jointly handled

---

[2] Chungshe consists of thirteen "neighborhoods." For most social, economic, and ceremonial purposes, however, the village includes only eight neighborhoods centered around the village crossroads.

by the headman and his secretary. Chungshe also has a class of less permanent officials known as *t'ou-chia*, or "bosses." Once a year twelve "bosses" are selected by the village accountant to assume responsibility for the two major community festivals, *hsieh-kung yüan* (Festival of Thanksgiving) and *fu-tsu hsi* (Festival of Buddha). Care is taken to ensure that eventually every village male has a chance to serve in this position, whose duties are essentially to help collect household assessments and to provide labor during festivals. By divination, one of the twelve *t'ou-chia* is selected to serve as *lu-chu*, "Master of the Incense Burner," or ceremonial host.

Kinship and village administration. In Tatieh, as we have seen, agnatic affiliation plays little role in the selection of village officials. In Chungshe it has played a considerable role from the earliest days of the village, when one descent group (that of Lai Yüan) dominated community affairs. All eight headmen who held office prior to 1945 were members of the dominant lineage, and all resided in the village "head." Five belonged to the wealthiest subbranch of the Lai Yüan group. By contrast, of the five headmen who have served since Restoration, only one has been drawn from the Lai Yüan group, two have had surnames other than Lai, and all five have resided in the village "tail." This striking change, and the more rapid turnover of headmen since 1945, reflects a precipitous decline in the importance of the job since the departure of the Japanese. Now that the headmanship is virtually devoid of power and prestige, it is no longer attractive to men of real influence.

Chungshe's village council was convened only twice during my year there, on both occasions to hear speeches and instructions from government officials. Neighborhood chiefs, like the headman, are reluctant captives of their office and apathetic toward their civic responsibilities. During one council meeting, for example, a villager came to complain that one Huang Ch'ing-liang, a 24-year-old immigrant to the community whose house was located on its outskirts, had been breaking bottles on the road in front of his house to prevent people from passing. The complainant asked the council to take action against Ch'ing-liang, but after a long discussion of the fellow's general lack of civic consciousness the matter was simply dropped and the complainant left the room grumbling.

On another occasion, when Lai Chao-hung filled in a public drainage ditch to make a road for his own convenience, I was told by several villages that he was "too strong" for this matter to be publicly discussed and arbitrated (he belongs to the wealthiest branch of the Lai Yüan descent group); they consoled themselves by predicting that heaven would punish him someday. Others, however, explained the inaction on the grounds that since Lai Chao-hung had stolen public rather than private property, no one was really interested. Chao-hung died of stomach cancer while I was still in Chungshe, and a number of villagers murmured about heaven's retribution.

In Tatieh, as we have seen, the headman plays an important role in the arbitration of interfamilial and intervillage disputes. He was concurrently head of the village corporation and he played a central role in public ritual. In Tatieh the headman was certainly more than a mere figurehead. He exerted considerable influence in his own right. In both villages, however, there has been a diffusion of influence and, in both, men of greatest influence are no longer interested in serving as headman. The weakening of this office is especially apparent in Chungshe. Disputes are more common in Chungshe, but the headman and village council play no significant role in their arbitration. This difference is due in part to the kind of people filling these offices, but it is also related to a long tradition in Chungshe of seeking decisions from *lao-ta*, or "big men," who are in effect the most influential members of major descent groups. Prestige and influence in Chungshe, as in Tatieh, have diffused somewhat since Restoration, but it is still from among the descendants of Lai Yüan that most leaders come and it is still to these leaders that villagers turn for arbitration. At the same time, real influence in the community has diffused just enough to make leadership of this sort less than fully effective.

Many disputes cannot be resolved within the village and must be referred to the courts. Acts contrary to the public interest often cannot be effectively dealt with. For retribution villagers either turn to the local police or simply look to the heavens.

As in Tatieh, every household is supposed to fulfill certain public responsibilities, but in practice such responsibilities are widely shirked. Although community clean-up drives are regularly announced, they are rarely carried out; and roadside drainage ditches in particular are constantly clogged with refuse. In Tatieh, major policy decisions are frequently made at voluntary meetings of household heads. Although two such meetings were announced while I was in Chungshe, both were canceled when only a few persons from the village "tail" showed up.

Internal challenge, external challenge, and community solidarity. Interfamilial disputes are commonplace in Chungshe, both between families of different surnames and between families of the same descent group. Many conflicts between families, especially families of the Lai Yüan descent group, are deep-rooted, and the most minor incidents bring them to the surface.

Although the dominant position of this group has never been contested within the community, struggles have erupted between it and lineages outside. About 80 years ago, for example, Lai Wen-fu, a descendant of Lai Yüan, owned a field bordering that of Lai Yün, a man from a different lineage who had recently moved into the village from Liuchia. When Lai Wen-fu attempted to cut some bamboo that Lai Yün had planted along the ridge separating their fields, the latter sought to prevent him. After a brief struggle in the field, Lai Yün was forced to retreat to Liuchia, where he asked for assistance from his relatives, one of whom was the village headman. When the headman came to discuss the matter with Lai Wen-fu, the latter lost his temper and tried to stab him. The headman returned angrily to Liuchia to round up some relatives who would return with him to Chungshe to punish Lai Wen-fu. When Lai Wen-fu got wind of the plan, he and his three cousins began to prepare ammunition and posted their tenants at the entrances of the village to watch for the enemy. At this point, government authorities were alerted and ordered the headman of Liuchia to call off his plans. Thus a struggle that had started out as an altercation between two individuals had rapidly escalated into a conflict between agnatic groups, not to mention a number of unrelated dependents on both sides. Government authorities, related to none of the parties involved, ultimately stepped in to mediate the dispute. Respected representatives of both descent groups were called together, and it was decided that Lai Wen-fu had been in the wrong. He was required to render an apology and pay compensation.

Another incident of the same period led to a confrontation between the progeny of Lai Yüan and the powerful Liu lineage that to this day dominates Liuying village to the north. One day Lai Ch'ing-t'ien became involved in an argument with two of his tenants, both residents of Liuchia, over some land rented by Lai Ch'ing-t'ien from a Liu landlord and subleased to these two farmers. When the two had attempted to deliver their rent directly to the landlord in Liuying, Ch'ing-t'ien stopped them and demanded that they pay the rent to him. The farmers subsequently reported to the landlord that Lai Ch'ing-t'ien wanted to appropriate the entire rent for himself. The Liu landlord promptly gathered a number of his agnates and went to Chungshe to confront Ch'ing-t'ien. When the band of armed men arrived in the village, they were met and driven off by a similar group rounded up by Ch'ing-t'ien. Help was summoned from Liuying, and a second confrontation took place on the banks of a nearby river in which Ch'ing-t'ien was killed and the Chungshe party forced to withdraw. The affair had now reached serious proportions. To prevent a major feud between the two lineages, government authorities intervened and arbitrated the matter. The Liu were obliged to pay 1.2 hectares of land to Ch'ing-t'ien's nephew as compensation for his death.

Although conflicts between descent groups were more common in the Chungshe area than in the Tatieh area during late Ch'ing times, they were still relatively infrequent compared to conflicts between descent groups and bandit gangs.[3] One such incident in particular is a favorite story of Chungshe's older villagers. Although my informants' accounts differed in detail, the general line of the story is clear.

In 1899 the ducks of a certain Ts'ai Hsiung, who lived in Shuilin village, and the ducks of Lai Sheng (of the Lai Yüan group) swam in the same pond. Ts'ai's ducks were repeatedly stolen and eaten by Chungshe villagers, but no one dared steal Lai's because of his family's powerful position. One day, Ts'ai demanded that Lai turn over half his flock on the grounds that their ducks had gotten mixed up. Lai refused, and Ts'ai left unsatisfied and angry. Some time later, Ts'ai approached Lai for a loan and was again rejected.

Ts'ai Hsiung eventually turned to banditry for a living. One night after midnight, he and his gang entered Lai Sheng's compound with the intention of forcing their way into his room and making off with his belongings. While they were breaking into his room, Lai Sheng and his brother Lai T'u fled to a section of the compound inhabited by their agnatic uncle Lai Shan-ho and his sons Lai T'iao-hsing and Lai T'iao-shou. Lai Shan-ho took up his gun and ran out to confront the bandits. More distant agnates living in an adjacent compound heard the firing and rushed to lend assistance. There were only five guns in the settlement at that time, all owned by descendants of Lai Yüan. Since other villagers had no weapons, and since they were not being attacked, they remained at home behind closed doors. The fight lasted several hours, and as daylight approached the bandits fled, taking with them a number of killed and wounded.

The following day, when some of the bandits went to Liuchia to have their wounds treated and to buy coffins for their dead comrades, they were seen by Lai Sheng and Lai T'u. The two brothers informed their uncle, who immediately formed a posse of his sons

---

[3] Conflicts along lineage lines, although uncommon, did sometimes erupt in Tatieh. One such struggle reportedly occurred in Tatieh during the final years of Ch'ing administration. As a result of an insult uttered in the heat of anger, two surname groups became involved in a street brawl that lasted for two days.

and nephews and some of their tenants. At his request, town officials allowed soldiers to accompany this force to Shuilin. Two of
the bandits were apprehended and dragged back to Chungshe,
where they were hung by their arms from a tree and beaten
severely. In the afternoon, they were taken to Hsinying (headquarters of the military police), where they died of their wounds. Ts'ai
Hsiung, furious because of his humiliation at the hands of the Lai
family, determined to get revenge.

Four months after this raid, an opera was staged in Chungshe
as part of a festival. A platform was erected near the center of the
village, and the gods were brought out to enjoy the performance.
Lai Shan-ho went out of his compound to purchase incense to
burn for the occasion. As he passed the platform he noticed men
ominously moving about in a field at the edge of the settlement,
and he subsequently recognized some bandits in the crowd of people gathered around the platform. Calling on villagers to seize
weapons and prepare for defense, he organized a number of tenants
into sentry shifts and stationed them at the entrances of the village. The bandits fled and did not return that night or the night
after. On the third day the sentries abandoned their patrols and
returned to their homes, assuming that the bandits had been
frightened off for good.

That evening, after everyone had gone to bed, the bandits returned in force. A few used ladders to scale the compound wall and
let their comrades in. Awakened by noises, Lai Shan-ho took up
his weapon and rushed out to find the bandits attempting to batter
down the doors of Lai Sheng and Lai T'u. The nephews were
afraid to come out, even though they had bought guns after the
first attack, and only Lai Shan-ho fired on the bandits. He was cut
down before anyone could come to his aid, and his two sons were
carried off as captives. Even then, with their uncle dead and their
cousins in danger, the two nephews failed to leave their rooms.
Their cowardice led to a major split within the descent group.
The ill will that was generated between cousins by this incident
has never healed; it has instead been exacerbated by subsequent
incidents. Lai Shan-ho's two sons were held for four months and

then they were released only after a sizable ransom had been negotiated and paid.

Although some parts of this story may be apocryphal, there can be little doubt that the raid took place. According to all versions of the story, furthermore, the community as a whole was at no point under siege. The objective of the bandits in this case (and in other cases as well) was to attack the Lai, the only wealthy descent group in the village and the only group living in fortified compounds. When violence broke out, other villagers did not rally to the Lai's support but withdrew into their homes. In effect, then, the dominant lineage, not the community, was both the principal target of attack and the principal unit of solidarity in organizing resistance. Other villagers were drawn in by virtue of their dependence on various Lai landlords, but they were essentially peripheral. It has always been so for the descendants of Lai Yüan, whether their conflicts have been with village dependents, other surname groups, or bandits. It is for this reason that, despite the history of factionalism within this group, it has been able to present a reasonably united front to challengers from the outside.

The community as an economic unit. In Chungshe, as in Tatieh, public expenses are provided for from the village treasury. The funds available to the community are derived from two sources—fixed assets and periodic assessments. The village collects rent on three publicly owned properties: the drying ground in front of the public meeting hall, an opera stage and the small piece of land on which it is erected, and two drainage ditches. As we have seen, part of one of these ditches was filled in by one of Lai Yüan's descendants to make a roadway for his own use; as a result, the village no longer derives income from it. In 1969 the community collected NT$1,700 in rent on the public drying ground and the opera stage land, which someone rented to pile straw, and NT$150 from pond owners for the use of public drainage facilities.

Clearly Chungshe has nowhere near as much public income as Tatieh. Nor has it any counterpart to Tatieh's "Make Prosperous Corporation." In 1968 the total fluid assets of Chungshe amounted to NT$7,702 (of which NT$1,839 constituted a carryover from

1967). After all expenditures for 1968 had been subtracted, the treasury had a surplus of NT$1,303. These figures demonstrate an almost total lack of interest in public enterprises apart from the separately funded festivals.

Association and community integration. Although social relations in Chungshe do cut across boundaries of neighborhood and kinship, they display nowhere near the range found in Tatieh. Most relationships are confined to the village, and the fact that agnates tend to live in clusters means that most of one's neighbors are also agnates. This is especially true in the village "head." Associations of the type so common in Tatieh are of little importance in Chungshe, and the membership patterns of what few there are reflect many of the basic divisions that mark the community.

In 1959 one Liu Shih, being desirous of promoting social intercourse among his fellow villagers, had the idea of creating an association for the worship of Chihwang. He talked the matter over with the god's medium, and the two men agreed on an association of 24 members—enough for a feast of three tables. In the end they could attract only seventeen. On joining, each member contributed ten catties of rice (worth about NT$20), and each is assessed a further NT$10 or so each year to help underwrite the association's annual feast. Moreover, each member in turn is expected to host the feast, which requires a further expenditure from his own pocket. The only monetary advantage to a member is the possibility of borrowing the association's fund in time of need.

Most members of the Chihwang Association are poor farmers who live in the village "tail." Although several surnames are represented, seven out of seventeen members are close agnates and two are related by marriage. Only eight members are related in no way at all. The Chihwang Association contains no members from the village "head," and none from the Lai Yüan descent group.

Curiously enough, in 1959 another Chihwang Society, formed in 1910, already existed in Chungshe. In purpose and activities, the two societies are similar; the big difference is that all the members of the older society are from wealthy families living in the village "head." Over half of its 40 original founders were descendants of Lai Yüan, and at least 35 of them had agnates within the group. That people from the "tail" had to duplicate this association rather than being able to join it says a lot about what kind of community Chungshe is.

The Fu-tsu Hui, or Buddha Society, was established in 1911 with an initial membership of 36. Its members still gather once a year for a feast, with each member serving as host in rotation. Between 1911 and 1940, new members paid a small initiation fee; the interest on the small fund was used to help offset the costs of the annual feast, with the host making up the deficit. The fund was lent to members at moderate interest.

In 1940, when the Japanese were building a police station and an elementary school in Chungshe and the Buddha Society was reportedly under considerable pressure for contributions, its members elected to disband and divide up the society's fund. Feasts and meetings were resumed after the war years, but the reorganized society has no funds. Members now contribute a "feast fee," and each host still makes up any deficit. Most current members are poor farmers from the village "tail"; the few that live in the village "head" are also poor. Half the original members were agnatically related to another member; and though the present membership reflects the multiplicity of surnames found in the village "tail," the percentage today is probably even higher, as it is in the similar Chuwang Society, founded in 1948. Only four members of the Buddha Society are descendants of Lai Yüan.

A Sungchiang Society, dedicated to the worship of a legendary general of that name, has existed in Chungshe since Ch'ing times. Since it has undergone three reorganizations, the present group is referred to as the "fourth generation." The original society was reportedly organized by wealthy members of the Lai Yüan descent group for "community defense" against bandits in the years just prior to the arrival of the Japanese. In fact its purpose was to defend the interests of wealthy Lai landlords. The society also had ceremonial functions: it staged martial exhibitions on festive occasions and was frequently called on to frighten away unwanted ghosts. Most of its 24 members were tenants of Lai landlords.

In 1910 a "second generation" society was organized. It seems that a drying ground in the abandoned compound of a wealthy Lai landlord was frequented by the ghost of a slave girl who had committed suicide there. When several villagers were frightened by this ghost while drying rice, the landlord decided to reorganize the Sungchiang Society in the hope that it would exorcise the ghost by performing martial exercises on his drying ground. With the help of contributions from among his wealthier agnates, he supplied weapons and other necessary paraphernalia. The group started off with 36 members and a fund of some 80 *yen* (from initiation fees), which was lent out at interest. Four villagers skilled in the beating of drums and gongs were enlisted to provide suitable accompaniment, and the group began its work by drilling every evening for two months. During this time their Lai benefactor, who was then also the village headman, ordered villagers to prepare snacks for them. In time, they became expert enough to earn money by giving exhibitions in other villages.

The second-generation Sungchiang Society lasted about 35 years. As older members died, they were replaced by their sons without payment of a new initiation fee. It is not entirely clear how and why the society dissolved. Some blame its demise on Japanese pressure; others hint that its funds were "eaten" (i.e. appropriated) by someone. In any case, the society was reformed in 1946 by Lai Shu-wu (a descendant of Lai Yüan) and Keng Lung-fang, a villager with newly acquired wealth. Although many villagers are said to have contributed to its formation, its 36 members soon developed irreconcilable differences and it was dissolved in 1948. The present "fourth generation" society was organized in 1967.

In 1899 seven families came to Chungshe from Touku, a nearby hamlet that was then disintegrating as a community because of disease and constant bandit raids. At the time of Touku's dissolution, over ten hectares of land belonged to the Wangyeh Society dedicated to that hamlet's god. Four of the Touku families that moved to Chungshe were cultivating three hectares of society

land. Shortly after they arrived in Chungshe, the Japanese conducted a land survey and registration and these three hectares of
land were listed as Wangyeh Society land. Only the seven Touku
families in Chungshe were recognized as shareholders, however.
Thus began, by a technicality, a new Touku Wangyeh Society,
with membership restricted to the seven families in question.
Each year, on Wangyeh's birthday, the members held a feast,
which they paid for out of rent profits. Feasts were discontinued
during the war years at the urging of Japanese authorities, but
were later resumed.

In 1936, when the four families cultivating this land wanted to
change its official designation from association land to privately
owned land, the other three families objected. It was finally agreed
that the land would be registered as "jointly owned" to protect it
from the Japanese, who were then putting pressure on all associations. This was a change in name only. Later, however, the land
was partitioned into seven equivalent parts and reverted to private property.

The descendants of the original seven member families have resumed their annual feasts despite the fact that they no longer have
an income-producing estate. Each member contributes ten catties
of rice and takes a turn as host. Members cooperate in many ways
(e.g. providing labor for funerals and weddings). Its members are
not so much citizens of Chungshe as outsiders with common interests and a common history. Significantly enough, they consider
their god more powerful than any other village deity.

In addition to its formal associations, Chungshe also has a variety of informal groups. About ten years ago for example, a few
villagers hired an instructor to teach them to play various folk
instruments. They then organized themselves as a band and hired
themselves out for weddings and funerals. The group finances two
feasts every year with profits earned in this fashion. Although most
of the villagers in this club are related agnatically or by marriage,
interest in music and not kinship was the important criterion of
membership. Neighborhood was also not an important consideration; the participants come from compounds scattered throughout
the village.

Several comparative observations can now be made with respect to associations in Chungshe and Tatieh. In 1935 Chungshe had only four corporate cross-kin associations, all with decidedly meager assets; Tatieh had 31 such associations, with landholdings totaling 97 hectares, not to mention an unknown but presumably large number of funeral associations and grain associations. Most of Tatieh's land-based associations had vanished by 1964, but there remain a variety of associations that possess sizable funds in cash or kind; Chungshe, by contrast, had only five such associations in 1968 and their assets were negligible. In composition, Chungshe's associations have reflected the internal divisions that mark the community—between rich and poor, "head" and "tail" residents, landlords and tenants, Lai families and others. Membership in Tatieh's associations, on the other hand, is typically village-wide and reflects no such cleavages.

Ritual and community. Although most of Chungshe's societies, like those in Tatieh, have a religious function, they have not served to unify the community in terms of common religious goals. All villagers worship Chihwang, for example, and yet there are two Chihwang associations, one for the rich and one for the poor. All villagers also worship Chuwang and Kwanyin, but only certain kinds of people belong to the Chuwang and Buddha societies. Though religious behavior in Chungshe does to some extent promote a sense of community, it is also used to emphasize distinctions within the village.

Originally there was no temple in Chungshe to serve as a focus of village unity; the gods were housed in various private homes. In 1899, as the fortunes of Touku hamlet declined, Lai Shan-ho, a descendant of Lai Yüan, persuaded some of its inhabitants to move their temple and god to Chungshe. The Touku temple was torn down, and the materials were used to build a small temple in Chungshe. In 1944 this primitive structure was replaced by a larger one, which was called not a temple but a "public meeting hall." In 1967 this wooden structure was replaced by a new "public meeting hall" built of brick and concrete. The new building, which consisted of one small room, was jointly financed by the government, the village treasury, and voluntary contributors.

Compared to Tatieh's temple, with its courtyards, bedrooms, towers, and temple paraphernalia, Chungshe's hall is a decidedly unimpressive structure. Except on festivals and occasions when it is needed as a meeting place, its doors remain locked. Few villagers contribute to its maintenance, and most speak of it as a public room in which the gods are kept rather than as a temple. Perhaps this is why on wedding days, when Tatieh villagers carry sacrifices to their temple, Chungshe villagers prefer to carry the gods to their sacrifices.

Whatever the reason, the pattern is clear: in Tatieh people are quick to visit the village temple, in Chungshe people tend to stay home. On the first and fifteenth of each lunar month, for example, when Tatieh villagers visit the temple to worship their gods, Chungshe villagers worship the gods and hungry ghosts in their own homes. In Tatieh, a few villagers take their problems to the temple every evening, and regular worship is conducted there twice a day. In Chungshe, the "public meeting hall" remains locked for weeks on end.

In Chungshe, as in Tatieh, a number of ceremonial activities affect all households at the same time. Chief among them are the New Year, the Festival of Buddha, the Third Day Festival, the Chuwang Festival, the Chihwang Festival, the Festival of Hungry Ghosts, and the Harvest Festival. In Chungshe, however, these events are largely seen as household rather than community affairs.

All New Year's events, for example, are conducted within the household or the compound; temple deities are not worshiped, and no public sacrifice is presented before the Heaven God. There is no event in Chungshe comparable to Tatieh's Making Happiness Festival, which, as we have seen, involves considerable coordination and expenditure at the community level. The Festival of Buddha, which occurs on the seventh day of the second month, is a more public affair, involving considerable coordination at the village level and extensive feasting of friends and relatives from outside the community. Yet even at this festival, the most important in Chungshe, there are no public and private sacrifices comparable to those that Tatieh people present at their village temple during the analogous Matsu Festival. During the festivals in honor of Chuwang and Chihwang (which occur in the fourth and sixth months, respectively), only some families carry a sacrifice to the public meeting hall, and only for the second of these festivals is a small public-financed sacrifice provided.

As in Tatieh, the Festival of Hungry Ghosts occurs in the middle of the seventh month. Once again each household simply provides a sacrifice for the ghosts in its own courtyard; sacrifices are not carried to any central place, and no sacrifice is provided by the community as a unit. *San-jih chieh*, the Third Day Festival, which corresponds to the Festival of Graves in Tatieh, follows the same pattern. On the second day of the third month, villagers worship the hungry ghosts in their courtyards, and the next day they offer sacrifices to the ancestors in their compound halls. For the most part, only wealthier families of the Lai Yüan lineage and representatives of Lai lineage branches with ritual responsibilities visit the ancestral graves. Since many of Chungshe's tombs are scattered about on private fields, there is no public gathering in the graveyard.

Of particular interest in Chungshe is a festival known as *hsieh-kung yüan*, or "Festival of Thanksgiving," which is held during the eleventh month to express gratitude for the harvest. During the afternoon, villagers carry sacrifices to the public meeting hall. In the evening the households of the village "head" are responsible for preparing a sacrifice to the God of Hell, and after midnight those of the "tail" provide a sacrifice for the Heaven God and his heavenly host. A ritual specialist is hired to conduct both ceremonies, and a sacrifice is also provided by the public treasury. What is interesting is that only a few villagers actually attend these ceremonies. Although they are organized at the community level to perhaps a greater extent than any other village ceremony except the Festival of Buddha, their organization clearly reflects the basic division of the community into "head" and "tail," and it is in these terms, rather than as a village-wide activity, that the festival is perceived.

FIVE

Sources of Variation

TATIEH'S SOLIDARITY has been achieved by emphasizing association and playing down patrilineal affiliation within the community. The importance attributed to cooperation within the village and between neighboring Hakka communities is evident on
every hand. It is even reflected in the kind of corporate lineages to
which villagers once belonged, structures that functioned to merge
agnatic groups rather than to discriminate between them. In
Chungshe there has been no comparable stress on ways of unify-
ing the community or reinforcing alliances between communities.
Chungshe's lineages are the product of a segmentary process, and,
unlike many of Tatieh's, they are largely confined to the village.
What accounts for these differences in emphasis? In this final chapter, we shall consider the impact of four possible factors—namely,
urbanization and industrialization, ethnicity, Japanese colonial
policy, and the nature and conditions of initial settlement.

The Urban Influence

The notion that urbanization, industrialization, and Western-
ization disrupt traditional kinship structures and affiliations is im-
plicit in much of anthropological literature, often without the benefit of solid empirical justification. The literature on China is no
exception (e.g. Chen Shao-hsing 1956: 2; Hu 1948: 98–99). In particular, there is a tendency to presume that where the functional
importance of kinship has clearly altered or diminished, the
change is a direct consequence of pressures introduced by industrialization and urbanization. A related presumption is inherent

in the tendency to think of areas beyond the city in terms of the
city, a tendency that Jones (1955: 40) has aptly labeled "intellec-
tual urbanism":

A current thought convention is that which identifies people, institutions,
and economic-social organization with a locality center rather than as
being located in space. From this point of view emphasis is placed upon
the influence of the center to the extent that there is the conclusion that
areas about the center are taking on the characteristics of the center. The
other point of view is that in which a point is selected on the historical
continuum and used as a measure by which to assess the behavior patterns of people, institutions, and economic-social organization of a different time period. Selection is made of a general period on the historical
continuum and a rural area is proved to be different now from what it
was then.

With these warnings in mind, let us consider the possible influence of urbanization and industrialization on Tatieh and Chungshe. An interesting case for comparative purposes is pre-Communist Nanching, the Kwangtung village described by C. K. Yang
(1959b). This village resembles Tatieh and Chungshe in size of
population, number of households, crop preferences, and multilineage character. Moreover, despite Nanching's long contact with
the industrial and urban complex at Canton, five miles away, it
continued to retain an essentially "rural" character. But it also
differs from Tatieh and Chungshe in important respects. More so
than either Taiwan village, Nanching was a community in which
agnatic principles prevailed. Beyond "tightly knit" kinship organizations, villagers "contracted few direct and intimate social
bonds" (p. 81). Although whatever urban and industrial influence
did exist had more impact on the descent group than on the immediate family (p. 88), lineages were still active and viable when the
Communists arrived in the village.

Can the differences between Nanching, Tatieh, and Chungshe
in the importance of agnatic affiliation be attributed to differences
in the impact on these communities of disruptive forces emanating
from an industrial-urban center? Before examining this question,
let us determine when and how rural Taiwan, and Tatieh and
Chungshe in particular, came under the influence of such forces.

Despite the general economic accomplishments of the Japanese on Taiwan, the social and cultural patterns of the Taiwanese were little affected by their presence. As Barclay summed it up (1954: 42), "What the Japanese themselves referred to as the 'industrialization of Taiwan' was nothing but a corporate superstructure placed on an agrarian base. This was not capable of diffusing an industrial culture thoroughly among the general population, because it had been devised to prevent this very thing." It would appear, furthermore, that the migration of Taiwanese to cities during the Japanese period did not lead to their absorption in an urban culture, nor was it associated with any significant culture feedback to the rural areas (Barclay 1954: 132).

Tatieh and Chungshe conform perfectly to Barclay's pattern. The nearest city and industrial complex of any importance to Tatieh in Japanese times was Kaohsiung, 44 kilometers to the north. The major city nearest to Chungshe was Tainan, 35 kilometers to the south. Though a few villagers from each community left to seek employment or schooling beyond the elementary level, the Japanese census for 1935 found less than 2 percent of Tatieh's total registered population, and 0.2 percent of Chungshe's, temporarily absent (*Kuo shih* 1937: 92–93, 130–31). Most of both villages' surplus products were taken from them in the form of taxes and rents, and visits to market centers were accordingly infrequent. Travel abroad was restricted by the Japanese prior to the outbreak of war with China in 1937, and was virtually impossible during the war. Even contacts with local Japanese were limited, since no Japanese resided permanently in either community. No matter where they lived, moreover, the Japanese managed to segregate themselves from the Taiwanese.

It would seem, then, that the enormous difference between Nanching and Tatieh in the importance of agnatic affiliation, and the lesser difference between Tatieh and Chungshe, cannot be explained simply in terms of industrial or urban impact. In Nanching, despite long and intimate contact with a huge industrial-urban complex only five miles away, agnatic affiliation continued to play a major role in community integration. And although Ta-

tieh had no more intimate contact with urban centers than Chungshe, the two villages differed remarkably in the importance attributed to agnatic bonds.

The Ethnic Factor

What about ethnic factors? Is it possible, for example, that
strong localized agnatic groups and loose community integration
are characteristic Hokkien features, while an emphasis upon association and firm community integration is characteristically Hakka? Or perhaps that the differences between the two communities
reflect adaptations to divergent mainland conditions, adaptations
that were then carried over to Taiwan? Ethnic differences clearly
played some part: during Chungshe's pre-Chianan phase, for example, Hokkien reluctance to put women into the fields exacerbated labor shortages at critical points in the agricultural cycle.
But as we have already seen in connection with our discussion of
family form, common ethnic origin does not invariably lead to
identical forms of social organization. By the same token, we often
find similar social phenomena among different ethnic groups. Although we cannot rule out an ethnic contribution to the differences between Tatieh and Chungshe, there are strong grounds for
believing that ethnic origin has not been crucial.

Pratt's description of Chong village (1960), a Hakka community
in the New Territories, shows that Hakka ethnicity does not inherently obstruct lineage elaboration. Chong village contains 40
families, all of which form a single lineage. Although a great many
villagers are employed in Kowloon or overseas, lineage development has been carried much further there than in Tatieh; for
example, Pratt reports segmentation and ritual nesting within the
descent group. That the three "sections" of the lineage are residentially discrete and have separate lineage halls indicates that at
one time the group possessed a measure of corporate wealth (1960:
148–49).

Or consider Hsin Hsing, the Taiwanese farming village described by Gallin (1966). In terms of lineage organization, this
Hokkien community resembles Hakka Tatieh more closely than

Hokkien Chungshe. Lineages are structurally simple and economically undeveloped (pp. 112, 131–32), and nonagnatic bonds are widely exploited. Relationships crosscut kinship and village lines. Unrelated families participate in funeral societies, grain associations, sworn brother groups, and the like (pp. 28–29). Subsistence activities especially require extensive cooperation between families across agnatic lines (pp. 172–73, 175ff). According to Gallin, the relative importance of friends and affines in the economic life of Hsin Hsing villagers has seriously undercut the solidarity of agnatic relations (p. 135).

K'un Shen, the Taiwanese Hokkien fishing village described by Diamond (1969), is also more like Tatieh than Chungshe. Although the ancestors of K'un Shen's 3,000 inhabitants came from a region of China where lineage organization and function are highly elaborated, and although many of its lineages contain more households than those in Chungshe, agnatic organization is not as well developed. None of the descent groups in K'un Shen maintains a genealogy, none has an ancestral temple, none convenes to worship common ancestors, and none owns corporate land (p. 68). As a matter of fact, K'un Shen's lineages "function mainly as religious cults" in which membership is not limited to agnates (*ibid.*).

In terms of lineage organization, then, K'un Shen is more like Tatieh than Chungshe, and the two are alike in other respects as well. Many of the associations found in Tatieh (and not in Chungshe) have counterparts in K'un Shen (pp. 23, 46, 77). Like Tatieh, K'un Shen is a "temple community." According to Diamond, "the strongest organizing force in the village is its main temple," which is administered by an elected committee of twelve prestigious individuals, four from each of the village's three neighborhoods (p. 78). Like the directorate of Tatieh's "Make Prosperous Corporation," this committee manages considerable property in the community interest (p. 78).

In the pattern and importance of affinal relationships, K'un Shen also resembles Tatieh. One-fourth of the married women in K'un Shen were born and raised there; another fourth come from a neighboring fishing community with which villages have traditionally cooperated (p. 52). In addition to relationships based upon marriage and descent, bonds of friendship are of great importance (p. 74). In short, although K'un Shen is Hokkien, it has more in common with Tatieh than with Chungshe.

According to Freedman (1966: 95), "There is a great danger in the study of southeastern China that people will assume for all Hakka or Hokkien or Cantonese or Tiuchiu that what some of them do in one place is characteristic of the behavior of all of them." Yet even if we avoid this assumption as such, it is surely reasonable to suppose that immigrants to Taiwan, whether Hakka or Hokkien, would have recreated agnatic structures along lines that were familiar and ideologically preferred unless there were reasons for not doing so. Might it not be true that the particular Hakka who settled Tatieh and the particular Hokkien who settled Chungshe simply instituted the patterns of social organization of their respective mainland communities?

This explanation holds reasonably well for Chungshe, but does not work for Tatieh. All my information indicates that Tatieh's settlers were closely linked to the descent groups of their home communities; indeed, relations were maintained with lineages on the mainland through most of the Japanese period. There is no reason whatever to believe that the people who settled Tatieh were any less familiar with the model of a strong localized lineage than those who settled in Chungshe.

We find little in the sparse literature on the Kwangtung Hakka (or on the Hakka in general for that matter) to suggest that they were inherently different from other southeastern Chinese in the matter of social organization. According to the gazetteer for Chiaying *chou*, the Hakka there placed special emphasis on lineage branch affiliation; surname groups, large and small, were associated with ancestral temples, and in various cities clan temples were established by members of the same lineage living in different hsien (*Kuang-hsü* 1961: 8/2; see also Chang Fen-ch'ien 1960: 6–7). As was commonly the case in southeastern China, there was a tendency for Hakka lineages to be residentially segregated, and for villages to stress agnatic affiliation in their internal organization.

According to Chang Fen-ch'ien (1962: 65), "[The Hakka] lived together with other *tsu* relatives for defensive purposes. For this reason, the lineage was important to them and their lineages were unusually strong. Inner difficulties were resolved by lineage relatives, and offenses from without were settled by united force."[1]

The gazetteer reports that lineages and lineage branches of all sizes established ancestral estates (*Kuang-hsü* 1961: 8/7; see also Chang Fen-ch'ien 1960: 6–7). The way their profits were used and the nature of lineage ceremonial behavior both reflect the degree to which lineages and lineage branches were internally stratified.[2]

Although written accounts of the Kwangtung Hakka tend to be imitative, overgeneralized, and overidealized, eyewitness accounts confirm the essential points. During the early years of the Japanese occupation, a few Tatieh villagers had an opportunity to visit their ancestral villages on the mainland. In all cases these informants found single-lineage settlements with residentially segregated branches and multiple ancestral temples; lineages and lineage branches were corporate and functioned as ceremonial units. It would appear, then, that we must look elsewhere for an explanation of the differences between Tatieh and Chungshe.

The Japanese Influence

Within the short period from 1935 to 1952 (see Tables 16 and 17, pp. 74, 75), the number of corporate descent groups to which Tatieh villagers belonged decreased from 21 to six, and corporate holdings of cultivated land fell from 134 hectares to four. There

---

[1] See also Chang Fen-ch'ien 1960: 6 and 1962: 60, 65, 86; D'Estrey 1890: 96; Hsieh 1929: 204; and Kuo Shou 1963: 30.

[2] Lineage properties could include more than temples and cultivated land. For example, claims were also asserted over grassland (Paton n.d.: 25). The annual income from ancestral properties, according to the gazetteer, was used to pay the costs of ancestral sacrifices, to provide for the poor and infirm, to reward parents who sent their children to prepare for civil service examinations in the ancestral temple, and to subsidize students. Since the security and prosperity of a lineage to a large extent depended upon its ability to produce scholars and officials, special attention was given to education. According to Chang Fen-ch'ien, some lineages with particularly large estates established elementary or middle schools for children "of the same surname" (1962: 74; 1960: 6–7).

was no comparable development in Chungshe. In 1935 Chungshe villagers belonged to twelve lineage corporations owning 23 hectares of land; in 1968 there were still ten corporations owning twenty hectares. We might well wonder what happened in Tatieh, and why the same thing did not happen in Chungshe.

For one thing, the onset of the war with China in 1937 brought intense new efforts to rid the Taiwanese of Chinese customs, which were seen as potentially subversive, and convert them to Japanese ways. The late 1930's, therefore, were a time of name changing, idol smashing, and even Japanicization of dress.[3] Among the Chinese institutions that got caught up in this assimilative fever were lineages and corporate associations. Corporation managers in Tatieh were frequently summoned and urged to push for dissolution. Police officers regularly attended corporation meetings to ensure that subversive activities were not being planned. Corporations were pressed to buy government bonds and to make contributions of all sorts. It was rumored that the Japanese intended either to confiscate corporate properties or to take over their management (and thereby eliminate the distribution of profits). The result of these pressures and rumors was a sudden flurry of land sales. It is clear from documents and from what older villagers told me that nearly all of Tatieh's corporations (kin and cross-kin alike) were dissolved between 1935 and 1940. After 1940, meetings were no longer held and profits were no longer distributed.[4]

Despite the ample opportunities offered by Taiwan for the accumulation of wealth (and therefore for the endowment of lineage

[3] The policy proved a complete failure, as had earlier Japanese efforts at assimilation (see Ballantine 1952: 47–48).

[4] Japanese pressures of this sort were by no means unique to Tatieh. I have heard accounts of similar pressures in Pingtung city, Chiatung, Neipu, Tainan, and Meinung. According to Tatieh villagers, those corporations that survived the war years were gradually dissipated through indifference and corruption. Because of wartime problems and dislocations, people had little time for lineage affairs. Meetings were not held. Tenants on corporate properties refused to pay their rents, and earnings dropped sharply. As the number of persons with a legitimate claim on lineage funds increased, dividends dwindled and conflicts became more frequent, together with accusations of manipulation and corruption. In short, as lineage membership became less advantageous, divisive forces that had previously been kept in check came to prevail.

trusts), comparatively few strong localized lineages have developed on the island. The Japanese occupation and pressures exerted upon developing lineages during the war undoubtedly discouraged the full elaboration of agnatic structures (cf. Gallin 1966: 130); in this respect there is merit to the relationship proposed by Freedman (1958 and 1966) and Potter (1970) between strong government and weak lineages. Yet we must still explain why those Taiwanese lineages that did emerge did not all develop in the same way or to the same extent. Why, for example, did lineages yield more readily to Japanese pressures in Tatieh than in Chungshe? Inferences from the structure of corporate descent groups in Tatieh and from the little we know of the pre-1937 period strongly suggest that the functional importance of agnatic structures had been seriously compromised by affiliations of a cross-kin type even *before* the Japanese applied their pressures. This may have contributed significantly to the more precipitous decline of descent group corporations in Tatieh in the late 1930's, not to mention the absence of any effort to rebuild them after 1945.

The Role of the Frontier

Freedman has speculated on a possible relationship between the uneven distribution of strong localized lineages in China and several other variables—namely, the conditions of frontier life, irrigation, and rice cultivation. On the frontier, he notes (1966: 163), cooperation was necessary not only to bring virgin land under cultivation but for defense. Among frontiersmen with a patrilineal ideology, this need for cooperation might well have stimulated the development or redevelopment of lineage structures. Another important factor was the agricultural surplus normally generated by a rice economy; it was this surplus that initially made possible the establishment of corporate estates, which in turn promoted the development of large agnatic communities (Freedman 1958; cf. Potter 1970 and Anderson 1970). Given a corporate focus, developing lineages could then take upon themselves legal, political, and defensive functions. Finally, the "mature and productive irrigation works" so intimately linked to the southeastern Chinese rice economy also probably stimulated a high incidence of collective lands (Freedman 1958: 160; 1966: 160).

Freedman has provided some interesting case material illustrating how ambitious local irrigation (and land reclamation) projects *may* become a function of the descent group, and how some cooperative endeavors of this sort have led to the establishment of descent group estates. Yet his formulation has its difficulties. First of all, though one might readily expect agnates to cooperate in building an irrigation pond on adjacent fields *belonging to them*, as was done in Chungshe, what happens when a canal must be built through the fields of nonagnates or even through the territory of other communities? In addition, maintaining and operating irrigation facilities (both on the frontier and in more developed areas) may require a different kind of cooperation from the one-time cooperation involved in building them. Exactly what kind depends largely on the nature of the irrigation system and the way land in that system is distributed. Irrigation and cultivation in the Tatieh area, for example, have always required extensive cooperation across descent group lines, whereas in the Chungshe area during the pre-Chianan period neither irrigation nor cultivation required this kind of cooperation. Cooperation in maintaining and operating local irrigation systems in no way precludes the formation of strong localized lineages; the point is simply that the two phenomena are not necessarily related. Indeed, cooperation with nonagnates in irrigation matters may well encourage such cooperation along other lines.

Again, although it is true, as Freedman indicates, that rice cultivation provides the potential for an accumulation of wealth and the endowment of estates, there must be some arrangement for making surplus production available for this form of investment and some reason for investing it in this particular way. In terms of land productivity, Tatieh was in a better position for such investment than Chungshe. Even though Tatieh's resources were more equitably distributed among surname groups, and even if no single surname group had a potential for investment in ancestral trusts comparable to that of the Lai in Chungshe, we know that families of the same surname in Tatieh did jointly contribute to endow ancestral estates. Yet the families with largest surpluses were instrumental in founding many of the village cross-kin associations and contributed heavily to their endowment. Although the overall productivity of Chungshe was lower, most of the potential for corporate investment was concentrated in the hands of the Lai families, and they used their resources almost exclusively for the building of localized ancestral trusts.

How are we to account for the concentration of wealth in the hands of Chungshe families, the lack of such concentration in Tatieh, and the fact that Chungshe villagers invested in ancestral trusts while Tatieh villagers split their investment? And why were Tatieh villagers interested in higher-order (i.e. nonlocalized) descent groups when Chungshe's villagers were not? Insofar as these questions can be answered, the answer seemingly lies in Freedman's third and most important line of explanation, the role of the frontier.

Here also, however, Freedman's tentative explanation has its problems. He speculates (1966: 164; cf. Potter 1970: 135–36) that "when settlement took place in rough frontier conditions, single lineage communities were likely to develop fairly quickly, and that when, in contrast, people moved into areas under firm government control, any initial agnatic heterogeneity in the incoming groups was probably perpetuated." In short, he argues that cooperation for local defense would be likely to take place primarily along agnatic lines in situations where immigrating family or lineage fragments, with little more in common than a "patrilineal ideology," found themselves thrust together for survival. It seems to me, however, that this is precisely what would not happen.

Let us consider the circumstances of the arrival of Han Chinese on China's southeastern frontier during T'ang and Sung times. According to Wiens (1954: 182), the Han settlement of most areas of Kwangtung took the form of military and commercial colonization; only after an area had been opened in this way did civilian migration become significant. Most migrants were not lineages but individuals or families in search of a new life (Freedman 1966: 11–12).[5] In time the increase in Han population in this region brought an increase in the amount and intensity of interethnic conflict (Wiens 1954: 187–90), presumably between an entrenched ethnic group and an initially less structured immigrant group. In these circumstances, the immigrants would presumably be more likely to form multilineage villages and cross-kin associations of various sorts than to choose the militarily weaker form of single-lineage villages and large corporate localized lineages. For purposes of offense or defense, multilineage communities might themselves be integrated into higher-order associations or alliances through the extension of kin (agnatic and affinal) and non-kin (ethnic, linguistic, or religious) bonds.

In the absence of an effective state force, then, Chinese in many frontier communities may have developed a more or less tribal form of integration.[6] The tribe, as Sahlins described it, consists of essentially similar parts (e.g. unspecialized multifamily groups that usually correspond to the residential and proprietary units of the tribe), which are loosely and mechanically integrated by a variety of pan-tribal institutions (e.g. clans, age grades, military or religious societies). The extent and form of a tribe's internal fusion or fission at any given time are a function of the sociocultural environment (Sahlins 1961: 326):

The existence of a well-organized predatory neighbor, or, conversely, the opportunity to prey upon a nearby society, will give impetus to confederation. Local autonomy breaks down, on a greater or lesser scale, proportionate to the amount of—and during the extent of—concerted action

---

[5] Eberhard summarizes the various migrations of the Wu clan in south China as follows (1962: 116): "Some persons move alone or with their closest family only, while others decide to make the move with friends or in-laws. Still others attach themselves to a larger emigrating group. Often migrations were made in waves: after one nuclear family has successfully settled, other families follow in the same or in later generations." Freedman remarks on the "fragmentary and heterogeneous nature of the lineage elements" migrating to certain parts of Nan Yang (1957: 24), and Cohen finds the same pattern in Hakka migration to Kwangtung (1968: 251).

[6] On societal levels as seen from an evolutionary perspective, see Sahlins (1961) and Service (1962).

possible against other societies. In an uncontested environment, on the other hand, the primary segments of a tribe will show little inclination toward consolidation. And if, at the same time, internal population growth places a premium on land, pasturage, or other vital resources, the tribe may exist in a virtual state of anarchy, of perpetual feud among small-scale segments.

Where Chinese frontier communities, or parts of different communities, came to be associated in higher-order (i.e. nonlocalized) agnatic organizations, such structures, generated for essentially offensive or defensive purposes, might have been initially produced as in Tatieh—by the aggregation of agnatic segments in different communities. Only in the absence of outside threats might population growth, increasing competition for strategic resources, and the production of agricultural surpluses combine to emphasize economic and kinship cleavages within and between territorial units. Only then would conditions be likely to encourage fission and the isolating kind of asymmetrical segmentation within descent groups that Freedman has brilliantly described.

If frontier conditions did in fact promote the formation of corporate localized lineages, we might expect some comparable development during the pioneering stages of Chinese overseas migration. Yet as Freedman notes (1966: 165), nothing of the sort has happened: "For the most part, urban conditions, non-agricultural pursuits in the countryside, and 'law and order' imposed by effective governments must soon have aborted any tendency for a traditional pattern of lineage grouping to emerge." Similarly, Freedman sees the absence of strong lineages in Hsin Hsing, the Taiwanese village studied by Bernard Gallin, as probably due to "its involvement in a modern system of economic life and communications" (1966: 99). As we have seen, however, the relatively weak development of localized lineages in many areas of Taiwan today can by no means be uniformly attributed to the impact of urban or industrial influences. And the same may be said of the impact of government activities on immigrants to Taiwan. Because of Ch'ing restrictions, much of the island's population growth was the product of illegal (and therefore undocumented) immigration.[7] Official regulations against immigration may therefore have delayed lineage development on Taiwan, but could scarcely have prevented it. Yet for the most part, and especially in those areas of the island where government control was *weakest*, localized lineages never did become greatly elaborated.

Although Chinese settlement of Taiwan goes back at least to the twelfth century, large-scale Chinese immigration to the island did not take place until the seventeenth. The flow of immigrants substantially increased with the arrival of Koxinga in 1661. Koxinga is said to have recruited some 30,000 soldiers from the Fukien coast during that year, and his son recruited another 6,000 three years later. Most of these soldiers were unmarried when they came to settle on Taiwan (Ta Chen 1923: 42–43). In addition, despite official restrictions, there was considerable civilian immigration to and migration within Taiwan. As local gazetteers show, whereas some migrant groups consisted of single families, or groups of patrilineally related kinsmen and their families, more consisted of unrelated households or groups of households.[8] As on the Kwangtung frontier, settlement in some frontier regions of Taiwan led to considerable ethnic rivalry and hostility (Chen Cheng-siang 1963: 48–49).

Official regulations undoubtedly exaggerated the heterogeneous nature of some frontier settlements on Taiwan, but the nature of migration in some areas of the mainland also encouraged heterogeneous settlement, as we shall shortly see. Taiwanese and mainland adaptations to comparable frontier conditions might there-

[7] For an excellent discussion bearing on the history, nature, and shortcomings of official attempts to restrict migration to Taiwan, see Chuang (1964). Other works of interest are Ch'en Ch'i-lu (1967), Chen Cheng-siang (1963), and Ta Chen (1923).

[8] The gazetteer for Miaoli county in north Taiwan, for example, relates that during the period 1796–1821, a certain Mr. Wu organized 84 *ku* (shareholders or partners) to open and cultivate land (*T'ai-wan* 1960: 51). In 1740, Messrs. Weng, Lin, and Chang, with the prior agreement of the aborigines in a certain locality, collected 20 or 30 farmers from Ch'üan-chou to cultivate land there (pp. 51–52). In 1751, Messrs. Wu, Wen, Huang, and Lo constructed housing for tenants who would open virgin land, and a settlement of 50 households was reportedly the result (p. 53).

fore be expected to have been generally similar. Some indication of what these adaptations might have been like is provided by materials relating to Hakka settlement in southwestern Taiwan.

According to one source, the main influx of Hakka from Kwangtung took place about 1686. They entered at the Hsia-t'an River and moved inland along its left bank, ultimately fanning out into the Pingtung plain. Since much of the plain was already occupied by Hokkien speakers whose ancestors had arrived earlier, the Hakka were restricted to a corridor roughly paralleling the mountains (see Map 6). They settled in close proximity to their Hokkien predecessors and either cultivated lands rented from absentee Hokkien landlords or opened new land, bringing water to it from nearby mountain streams and rivers. As their number grew, the Hakka found themselves competing with their Hokkien neighbors for land and especially for water. The danger of attack from them or from the Paiwan aborigines that inhabited the nearby foothills was always present (Liu n.d.: n.p.). As a result, Hakka of different surname and agnatic affiliation, too few in number to defend themselves, often gathered in villages around which they built protective walls (cf. Cohen 1969: 168). According to the Chinese sociologist Chen Shao-hsing, this pattern was common in Taiwan in the early days of settlement (1956: 4–5):

As the government was not strong enough to keep peace and order, self-defense was left to kinship groups or groups of people of the same native town. Under these circumstances the influental kinship group was very significant. It could defend its kinsmen better, it could suppress other groups and enjoy various privileges. Prosperous male kinsmen insured survival and prosperity, and this was the reason why an abundance of male descendants was the ideal life among the Chinese. The principle of blood relationship was very significant in this respect. On the other hand, however, for defense against raids of aborigines and bandits, even the influential clan had to get the cooperation of other people. This led them to stress territorial consolidation within the village.... Sociologically speaking, it is safe to say that, in spite of the often emphasized Chinese ancestral worship and family spirit, the principle of locality took precedence over the principle of blood relationship.[9]

    [9] In the late nineteenth century, similar conditions prevailed in the area of Hsin Hsing, a Hokkien village on the Changhua plain (Gallin 1966: 16): "The present area of Hsin Hsing was at that time the site of only a few scattered

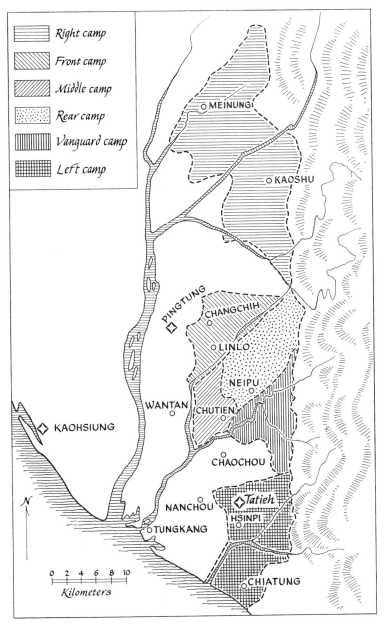

Legend:
- Right camp
- Front camp
- Middle camp
- Rear camp
- Vanguard camp
- Left camp

MEINUNG

KAOSHU

PINGTUNG

CHANGCHIH

LINLO

NEIPU

WANTAN   CHUTIEN

KAOHSIUNG

CHAOCHOU

Tatieh

NANCHOU   HSINPI

TUNGKANG

CHIATUNG

N

0 2 4 6 8 10
Kilometers

Map 6. Hakka distribution on Pingtung plain, 1933

Lineage corporations were early established in the Tatieh area to unite families of the same surname living in different communities. These organizations were useful in the event of conflicts with other descent groups, and at the same time provided an important means for uniting different communities in the face of ethnic hostility. To facilitate defense and cooperation among families of different surname, a variety of cross-kin associations were also formed. A precedent for such societies already existed on the mainland, but they assumed special importance in Tatieh because of its nearness to hostile Hokkien settlements.

Armed conflicts with these settlements—one of them a few kilometers north of Tatieh, another less than a kilometer to the west—were frequent and serious. Hostilities were usually precipitated by disputes about access to land, crops, or irrigation water; and lightning Hokkien raids on Hakka fields, particularly in the northern quadrants of the village, were frequent. Shortly before the advent of the Japanese, villagers owning fields in these areas organized a so-called *szu-chi hui*, or "Four Seasons Association," whose corporate profits were used to hire and arm guards to patrol members' fields. A *nan-hsing chieh hui*, or "South Happiness Street Society," was organized at about the same time to spare villagers the trip from Tatieh to Chaochou market, which, since the road passed through Hokkien territory, was not only physically inconvenient but dangerous. Formed with the idea of stimulating the development of commercial enterprises within Tatieh itself, the society extended loans from its fund to any villagers who would undertake to open shops on South Happiness Street. Nearly all village associations of that time had, in addition to their religious and social purposes, definite military or defensive functions.

Conflicts along lineage lines, although uncommon, did some-

---

households. The inhabitants were so few and so weak, and the bandits so many and so strong, that Hsin Hsing and eleven nearby villages formed a mutual protection association. When a village was attacked by bandits, it sounded large gongs as an alarm signal; the signal was relayed from village to village, and the able-bodied men rushed to the aid of the community under attack. The associated villages still maintain an informal organization today, though its function is now the production of a joint annual religious procession."

times erupt in Tatieh. Since Tatieh's lineages united families of the same surname within and between communities, in times of danger the aged and very young could be evacuated and sent to stay with agnates living in safer settlements. If necessary, armed men would be sent to distant agnates to assist kinsmen in Tatieh.

Confederation along ethnic lines on Taiwan was perhaps most vividly manifested in the famed *liu tui*, or "Six Camp," organization. Twenty or thirty years after the Manchus took Taiwan, their corruption precipitated a rebellion under the leadership of a Hokkien named Chu I-kwei, who claimed to be a legitimate descendant of Ming royalty. He was joined in his revolt by a Hakka leader, T'u Chün-ying. Later, an inner struggle arose among the rebels that resulted in a massacre of Hakka soldiers. The remaining Hakka forces fled south, where they created a new army by enlisting men from Hakka communities all over the Pingtung plain. This army was organized on a regional basis into six regiments or "camps" (see Map 6), and was placed under unified command. It fought with Ch'ing forces against the Hokkien rebels and was later reactivated to resist the Japanese (cf. Chung; Liu; and *Wan-luan* 1971).[10]

It is thus no accident that Tatieh residents frequently marry residents of adjacent Chiatung township, or that families in the two communities frequently exchange ceremonial and social visits. In pre-Japanese times, Hsinpi and Chiatung townships constituted a Hakka island surrounded by hostile peoples. Many families in the area could demonstrate recent agnatic connections dating back to the mainland; indeed, some may have chosen this particular area in order to be close to agnates or other Hakka already living there. In due course, relations between the communities of these townships were further deepened by the continuous proliferation of marital ties. Wanluan, Chutien, Neipu, and other Hakka areas to the north on the plain not only were farther away but were

[10] The "Six Camp" organization, although completely reorganized, still exists. It has lost its military function and now constitutes a Hakka religious, social, and political association. Hakka heroes are memorialized, stipends are provided for gifted students, and Hakka interests are generally guarded.

separated from Hsinpi and Chiatung by Chaochou, a Hokkien en-
clave. The intimate relations between Hsinpi and Chiatung were
recognized in the structure of the "Six Camp" organization; thirteen Hakka villages in the area were grouped together to form the
"Left Camp."

Before 1904 the nearest government force had been located as
far away as Pingtung city. In that year, however, having quickly
pacified the area, the Japanese established a police station in
Hsinpi village, and young men were selected from various communities in the township to form a local defense corps. Fighting
along ethnic and surname lines was all but eliminated, and one of
the major functions of corporate lineages and cross-kin associations accordingly ceased to exist.[11]

Tatieh's experience, then, suggests that far from fostering the
development of strong localized lineages, frontier conditions tended to inhibit such a development by requiring extensive cooperation for defense and environmental exploitation among unrelated
family and lineage fragments. Conversely, one might argue that
only where frontier conditions do not exist—where hostile forces
are not present and working the land does not demand extensive
cooperation with nonagnates—is a "patrilineal ideology" likely to
become dominant, as it did in Chungshe.

Although I have been able to locate few reliable documentary
sources for the history of Chungshe, oral traditions and the personal recollections of older men, however, agree on certain general
features. It appears, for example, that the aboriginal inhabitants
of this region had been cleared out by the military long before
any Chinese settlers arrived. Those Chinese who eventually did
settle in Chungshe, furthermore, were of similar mainland origin
and spoke the same dialect. It is likely, in other words, that set-

---

[11] Much the same thing apparently happened throughout Taiwan. According to Chen Shao-hsing (1956: 5–6), "After the colonial government began to
seek peace and order with its police and administrative system, kin groups and
local associations for self-protection and mutual aid gradually lost their raison
d'être. Gradually people became less eager to support these associations, and to
the young generation bred in peace and order, these associations became a
thing of the past."

tling in Chungshe involved considerably less risk than settling in Tatieh. Moreover, the Chungshe area offered an abundance of virgin land to all comers, and irrigation, as we have seen, required more cooperation from the gods than from men.

The differences in overall productivity between Tatieh and Chungshe may also help to explain their differential lineage development. In Chungshe, where water was less abundant and land less productive, there was less reason for settlers to compete for holdings; one family or group of families could settle and remain there in relative isolation without fear of being dispossessed by outsiders. Very possibly the early arrival of the Lai in Chungshe enabled them to establish a disproportionate control over village productive resources, which in turn induced them to distinguish themselves as a group from the dependent families that arrived later. The Lai investment in lineage estates may accordingly represent a projection of common economic interests—the interests of village "haves"—in a situation that placed no barrier in the way of expressing intravillage distinctions. Tatieh's land, by contrast, was more productive and at the same time controlled access to needed irrigation water; it was definitely worth fighting for, and for this reason could not have been defended by a small group of agnatically related households without outside help. From the beginning, access to the means of production in Tatieh seems to have been more equitably distributed among village families, and no ascribed status set the privileged off from the less privileged. In the face of a common outside threat, then, there was no obstacle to the merging of interests.

The main threat to the well-being of Chungshe's villagers came not from ethnic rivalry and competition but from bandit raids. In an attempt to discourage such raids, several Lai families (and *only* Lai families) constructed large, well-fortified compounds. When raids took place, Lai leaders organized the defense. Thus in 1880, when a bandit group occupied Shuilin and prepared for further incursions in the area of Liuchia, Lai Ch'un-ch'üan, the wealthiest and most influential person in Chungshe at that time, set about organizing resistance with the help of the village headman and the village *tung-shih* (whose function is unclear to me), both of them wealthy descendants of Lai Yüan. Whenever important decisions affecting the community had to be made, it appears that they were made jointly by the headman, the *tung-shih,* and several additional *lao-ta,* or important personages (invariably descendants of Lai Yüan).

Except for these sporadic and limited threats, which were soon dispelled by the Japanese, Chungshe seems to have been settled on a frontier characterized by relative peace. Not only were there neither hostile aboriginal peoples nor Chinese ethnic competitors, but until 1930 there was no significant competition for that most critical of resources, irrigation water, since fields for the most part were dependent on rainfall. In the circumstances, one numerically superior descent group came to dominate the village politically and economically from the very start, approximating in the course of time the Chinese model of a localized corporate lineage. No nonlocalized lineages of the sort found in Tatieh developed in Chungshe; there was no need for them. The nesting of lineage branches was segmentary rather than aggregative. Agnates within the descent group continuously distinguished among themselves in terms of the differential distribution of wealth within the group.

There is the possibility, then, that internally complex, localized lineages such as those in Chungshe are likely to emerge in uncontested frontier regions that have an economic potential for such development. As the larger population potential of paddy agriculture is realized and as the inhabitants of a village begin to use available land and water resources to their capacity, conflict within the village will increase. Given large populations of agnates, patrilineal affiliation might then serve as the chief basis for choosing sides within the village or between villages; thus Freedman asserts that "lineage alignments were the key to organized fighting" in southeastern China, at least as early as the eighteenth century (1966: 115). In this sense, lineage defense functions may account for the persistence of lineage strength in southeastern China until recent times. They do not necessarily explain the emergence of such lineages in the first place. In particular, it is not clear that the kind of lineages described by Freedman constituted a good key to fighting throughout southeastern China in the pioneering years.

Had it not been for Japanese pressures, technological innovations, and subsequent legal restraints upon the size of lineage estates imposed by the Nationalist government, Chungshe might have resembled Freedman's model of a strong lineage village even more closely. As it is, however, the likelihood is that as time passes Chungshe will more and more come to resemble Tatieh. Legal restraints limit the amount of land that individuals and lineages can accumulate, while subsistence activities increasingly require cooperation across agnatic lines. As villagers adjust to the growing need for such cooperation, the antagonisms generated during the land reform will probably be overcome and Chungshe may become a more cohesive entity.

Agnatic Variation in Southeastern China

In an effort to explain the different stress placed on agnatic kinship and nature of community integration in two Chinese villages in south Taiwan, we have singled out three factors as most significant: initial settlement pattern, the distribution of wealth, and the need for cooperation across agnatic lines for economic or defense purposes. These findings may have relevance for southeastern China generally. If we accept with Freedman that in China "the desire to form a single lineage in one territory is a motive given" (1966: 8), and if we assume a region with sufficient productive potential to make lineage formation possible, then, other things being equal, we might expect the following statements to hold.

1. Under frontier conditions, small agnatic groups are most likely to develop into single-lineage communities where competition for subsistence resources is minimal.

2. In multilineage communities, a need for cooperation across agnatic lines for economic or defense purposes (or both) works to inhibit the structural elaboration of localized lineages, especially where families exert more or less equal control over subsistence resources.

3. Higher-order (i.e. nonlocalized) descent groups resulting from an aggregative process are likely to appear in situations where territorially discrete and numerically weak agnatic groups are aligned within the framework of a cohesive territorially based organization that has been formed to confront a large and persistent common enemy.

In *Chinese Lineage and Society* (1966), Freedman considers the relationship between settlement pattern and patrilineal grouping in China. One opinion often expressed (pp. 5–6) has been that multilineage communities and meager lineage elaboration result from the breakup of single-lineage communities, which are accordingly seen as historically prior to mixed settlements. Freedman points out that a reverse sequence is also possible, that multilineage settlements have become single-lineage communities when one agnatic group succeeded in driving other groups out or when all but one lineage died out (pp. 6–13). There are several ways, according to Freedman, in which multilineage settlements can get started. They may result from a "gathering together of elements pushed out of communities by oppression," or when outsiders gain a foothold in lineage territory as tenants (pp. 13, 8). Bearing in mind, then, that shifts in both directions are possible, let us see whether our three-point hypothesis suggests any general trends for southeastern China that might help us to a better understanding of the relationship between lineage and settlement pattern there.

It would appear that under certain circumstances—namely, on uncontested frontiers with sufficient productive potential—single-lineage settlements were likely to have been favored and therefore historically prior to multilineage settlements. On relatively open and secure frontiers that provided little motivation for the repression of fissive tendencies within growing lineage communities, agnatic groups might send members out to establish independent communities elsewhere.[12] Multilineage communities probably often emerged in frontier settlements where small agnatic groups

---

[12] Hsiao cites a case from Chihli province, for example, where 24 single-lineage villages were scattered about the landscape (1960: 324; see also p. 327): "From the fact that most of [the inhabitants of] these villages had the same surnames and that most of these inhabitants bearing identical surnames belonged to the same clans, it may be gathered that at the beginning there were

of diverse provenance found themselves competing for resources with well-entrenched predecessors. As population built up and as new immigrants added to mounting pressure on resources, larger communities and alliances between communities would afford rational adaptations. The more formidable and persistent the threat, the more persistently small agnatic groups or small communities would seek to forge alliances.[13]

Intercommunity alliances could be facilitated and bolstered by emphasizing or even conjecturing common descent (see Hsiao 1960: 352–54). Although descent groups of this sort constitute only one mechanism for reinforcing and giving continuity to alliances, this device would be especially suitable among kinship-oriented peoples. It may also be that the more persistent and well-defined the enemy—as, for example, where adversaries are identified in terms of language—the greater the likelihood of higher-order agnatic structures. Such structures clearly served to unite Hakka villages on the Pingtung plain of Taiwan, and examples can be found on the Chinese mainland as well (Hsiao 1960: 422).

On the basis of documentary materials, Cohen (1968) recently demonstrated that language differences have significantly influenced the alignment of social groups in Kwangtung and Kwangsi provinces. He noted that Fukien and Kwangtung, the two provinces of China with the highest incidence of villages dominated by a single lineage, were also a region of considerable linguistic heterogeneity (pp. 238–39). Conflicts along language lines became particularly important in this region during the mid-nineteenth century.[14] By Cohen's account, Hakka settlement in Kwangtung and Fukien was remarkably similar in pattern to Hakka settlement on the Pingtung plain of Taiwan. In both cases, small groups of ag-

---

only a few households which, owing to their poverty, went without authorization into the hills and reclaimed the land. As time went on, a number of villages were gradually formed."

[13] Hsiao describes two cases of alliance building during the mid-nineteenth century (1960: 366–67, 343). One case involved recently settled Hakka communities that refused to pay rent for a market leased from a powerful Cantonese lineage; in 1850, after six years of fighting, 90-odd Hakka villages united to exterminate their common enemy. In the other case, several neighboring Cantonese lineage communities allied themselves to resist recent Hakka settlers.

[14] Reminding us that it was not until the Sung period that lineages began to

nates arrived and settled where they could; in both cases, the Hakka became more of a handicap than an asset to their predecessors as their population grew (cf. Cohen 1968: 248). Confronted by larger and more powerful communities of Cantonese, the Kwangtung Hakka, like their counterparts on Taiwan, found it advantageous to join efforts for strategic reasons (p. 260).

As on Taiwan, Hakka consolidation on the mainland took place in stages. First there was a banding together of small agnatic groups into multisurname communities where terrain made it possible (pp. 260–64).[15] Next on Taiwan came alliances between communities, and there is evidence of similar alliances on the mainland (pp. 267–70). Because Hakka communities were frequently multisurname in composition, higher-order lineages linking small groups of the same surname in different villages would have provided, as they did on Taiwan, an effective means of ensuring continuity to the alliances between villages. It is also reasonable to suppose that within communities composed of small and disparate agnatic groups, the same threat that led to intercommunity alliances would encourage association between groups and a playing down of agnatic differences.

According to Freedman, higher-order lineages are typically formed by the dispersion of surname groups in different localities; that is, they are nonlocalized manifestations of the same kind of segmentary process that takes place within localized descent groups (1966: 37). There is some evidence, however, that higher-order descent groups need not invariably involve groups that are offshoots of a single parent community, that they may be created by simply inventing common ancestors to serve the purpose at hand (cf. Hsiao 1960: 352–54). There is an important difference between

---

assume their present form, Cohen (1968: 242–43) suggests a relationship between the sudden attention given to keeping genealogies and the intensified absorption of non-Han groups then taking place in southeastern China. There may have been, in other words, a relationship between lineage formation and inter-ethnic fighting.

[15] The interspersed settlement of Hakka on less fertile land was not conducive to an immediate clustering of large groups of people. The Cantonese, by contrast, had both better land and sufficient time to grow in number and develop communities of this sort (cf. Cohen 1968: 252–53, 267; Freedman 1966: 36; and Potter 1968: 12).

higher-order lineages formed on the basis of aggregation and those that develop through segmentation. In the former, distinctions within the group are deemphasized; in the latter, distinctions are stressed.

Freedman has been especially interested in demonstrating a fit between descent group structure and socioeconomic stratification in China; as he shows, it is the differential accumulation of wealth within the descent group that accounts for the asymmetrical nature of lineage segmentation. This finding, which has been generally confirmed by Baker (1968) and Potter (1968; 1970), is in no way incompatible with my proposition that under certain circumstances higher-order lineages can be produced by a process of aggregation, whose primary purpose is to include rather than exclude members. In such instances, system asymmetry may reflect (as it did in Tatieh) the distribution of local descent groups on the ground more than differentials of wealth. Nearby groups that wish to link up discover a common "ancestor" through whom they may be connected; they in turn can find "ancestors" further removed through whom they can link up with more distant or more numerous groups, etc. In the end they produce a structure that resembles the asymmetrically segmented descent group but that is functionally more like the kind of lineage described by Sahlins (1961).[16]

If the suggestions I have made here have any general value, the data contained in other community studies of Taiwan and south-

[16] There is an interesting parallel between Nuer expansion in Africa and Hakka expansion in China. In discussing Nuer expansion into Dinka territory, Sahlins asks why the Dinka did not, like the Nuer, have a segmentary lineage system, but instead lived in small and relatively independent local units (1961: 340): "This difference between Nuer and Dinka is, we think, related to differences attending their respective occupation of the Sudan. The Dinka appear to have spread without great opposition. *They were first.* They naturally grew by segmentation, and fissioning units could, in the absence of external threat, afford to organize as small, virtually self-contained entities. The Dinka themselves suppose that small settlements inevitably grow and break up into discrete groups, each able to stand by itself." The Cantonese, with their strong, localized, and relatively independent agnatic groups, were also "first." The Hakka were second, and thus were forced to consolidate small agnatic fragments into larger, more effective units. One means of consolidation was higher-order lineages.

eastern China should at least not be inconsistent with them. Several such studies have been carried out in regions of China where, in Freedman's terms, the productive potential for an emergence of strong localized lineages was present. Let us see what these studies have to say about the conditions under which such lineages did or did not emerge.

In Nanching (C. K. Yang 1959b), such lineages developed despite the multisurname composition of that community. The first ancestor of the oldest lineage (Lee) settled in Nanching in 1091. About a century later, a second lineage (Wong) settled there. The joining of two surname groups may have been a strategic accommodation—an attempt by two agnatic groups to consolidate their forces. Yang indicates that early settlers in Nanching had to "face the pressure of indigenous aboriginals" (*ibid.*). Then, as the Wong grew in number, "and as surrounding settlements closed in, they built dikes and filled in the shallow and rapidly silting river banks to create more land" (*ibid.*). In short, there was an increasing need for land from within the community, as well as mounting pressures from other communities.

In the face of growing competition from the outside, however, Nanching villagers did not follow the Tatieh course of deemphasizing differences in descent. Perhaps the major descent groups were already too large and developed to permit such a change; the Wong, for example, seem to have been sufficiently numerous to carry out on their own the reclamation project referred to above. Or perhaps the external threat was relatively insignificant. Whatever the reason, Yang's description of subsistence resources and activities in pre-Communist Nanching suggests that cooperation across surname lines was not important enough to offset the generally segmented character of the village.

In Phenix, the single-lineage village in Kwangtung studied by D. H. Kulp, the lineage was also asymmetrically segmented, the pattern of segmentation being expressed ritually and in terms of ancestral trusts (Kulp 1925: 145–46, 80–81, 101–2). Descent group membership was crucial to political and social life (pp. 135, 147). The few families in Phenix that did not belong to the dominant lineage occupied a distinctly dependent status; they did not participate in village ritual, and they were excluded from positions of leadership (pp. 117–20).

Unlike Tatieh, Phenix was not established by a few poor families of mixed surname. It was settled at the end of the sixteenth century, when a "whole kinship group was moved and established in its present location" (p. 68); from the very beginning, the dominant agnatic group was large and comparatively wealthy (pp. 68, 111).[17] There can be little doubt that the descent group played an important role in determining access to land (pp. 101–2). The village was settled long before the arrival of Hakka immigrants, and there seems to have been no threat from this quarter. Since strategic subsistence resources were lineage-controlled, there would have been no compelling incentive for consolidation across surname lines within the community. Phenix, then, was settled under conditions favorable for the expression of a patrilineal bias.

Like Chungshe and Phenix, the New Territories village of Sheung Shui (Baker 1968) is a community whose political, economic, ritual, and social life has long been dominated by a single descent group. The lineage is similarly localized and exhibits an elaborate nesting pattern; it is also the product of a segmentary rather than of an aggregative process. The founding of Sheung Shui resulted from a lineage consolidation (p. 29); in the seventeenth century eight Liao segments in proximal hamlets were brought together in one place (p. 172), presumably for defense against bandits and more aggressive lineages, both of which are known to have been active in the area. The Liao had to abandon Sheung Shui in 1662 as part of a government anti-piracy measure, but returned four years later (pp. 29–30). The new village built at that time was walled and consisted of four wards, each containing a lineage segment (p. 30). We find no mention of fighting along ethnic lines until the nineteenth century (p. 45). There was no apparent threat of sufficient magnitude to unite

17 At the time of Kulp's study, Phenix was still far from poor, to judge from his discussion of "slaves" (1925: 164–66) and his reference to "very large" profits from ancestral estates (pp. 86–87).

Sheung Shui with nearby villages in a continuing common cause.

Sheung Shui began, then, as a relatively populous and prosperous lineage community, presumably in a region consisting of similar communities (pp. 43–44). The Liao defended themselves not only against bandits and pirates but against nearby lineages, the very class of people to whom bridges were built in Tatieh. Nor was there any equivalent to the higher-order descent groups found in Tatieh and nearby villages; on the contrary, as Baker observes, "the expansionism of powerful lineages was so strong that not even common agnatic descent could prevent antagonism between neighbouring powerful lineages" (pp. 188–89). In sum, there was little need for cooperation between communities and little opportunity for cooperation across agnatic lines within the community, since one descent group controlled all important subsistence resources. The resulting social organization was almost purely patrilineal after the Freedman model.

Hang Mei (Potter 1968; 1970) is one of eight villages comprising the Tang lineage of Ping Shan in the New Territories. Unlike the dominant descent groups in Sheung Shui and Chungshe, the Tang are not confined to a single settlement. Although the maximal lineage is nonlocalized, it bears little resemblance to the higher-order descent groups to which Tatieh villagers belonged. It is a product of segmentation rather than of aggregation, and it is more elaborately segmented internally. As in Chungshe and Sheung Shui, the pattern of segmentation reflects differences in the accumulation of wealth and accomplishment within the descent group (1968: 18, 23–25; 1970: 126). Hang Mei's political and economic life is clearly dominated by, and predicated on, agnatic kinship (1968: 18, 27; 1970: 122–23). The settlement of Hang Mei exhibits strong parallels to the founding of Sheung Shui and Chungshe. Its founders claimed the best land; only later were they joined by other settlers, who had to content themselves with less desirable land or assume a status of inferiority and dependency (1968: 19–21).

Seemingly, then, strong lineages initially developed in Phenix, Sheung Shui, and Hang Mei because there was nothing to inhibit their development.[18] When competition for resources later became a factor, entrenched earlier groups attempted to exclude or dominate newer ones. It would not be surprising if further research in the New Territories turned up numerous villages more like Tatieh among later settlers—villages in which families of different surnames joined forces and played down agnatic differences for the sake of survival. It would be interesting to know, for example, whether the alliance of Hakka villages to which Baker refers (1968: 189) was made up of communities of this sort, and if their alliance was reinforced by higher-order lineages arrived at by a process of aggregation.[19]

Kaihsienkung (Fei 1939), in Kiangsu province, was a multi-surname community in which patrilineal descent groups were poorly developed. Fei's data suggest that the lack of lineage elaboration may, as in Tatieh, have been associated with a need for bridging surname lines. Beyond the family, says Fei (1938: 98),

the formation of larger groups depends on the common interests of those who live in a wider territory. For instance, there are natural menaces such as flood and drought and also the threat of invasion by an alien people, which do not affect single individuals but all those living in a

---

[18] Not only was there no entrenched enemy in these cases, but cooperation across agnatic lines has not been required for access to land or water, or for agricultural labor. In Sheung Shui, access to land and water was completely controlled by the lineage (Baker 1968: 164–65, 167). In Hang Mei the same is true (Potter 1968: 74, 96–101); moreover, "almost all the farm work is done by the farm family, and hired labor is not an important factor" (p. 75). In Nanching, it is hard to determine to what extent land access depended on agnatic affiliation; but irrigation evidently required little or no cooperation with non-kin (C. K. Yang 1959b: 26), and a combination of poverty and planting patterns made labor exchange almost impossible (pp. 38, 39).

[19] Baker mentions, for example, the Pat Heung alliance (1968: 189): "The Pat Heung alliance illustrates the difference between powerful and weak lineages, for it is an alliance of small lineages and settlements which are situated close together. Weak lineages, far from automatically repulsing their neighbours, were constrained to join with them as protection against more powerful lineages. In marriage ties they were confined no doubt to the standard marketing area; thus the whole range of their contacts and relationships operated within a small radius. Powerful lineages, on the other hand, as we have seen, tended to have few relationships in their immediate neighbourhood, but many outside it. Strong lineages could fight in their own defense and in offense: weak lineages had to content themselves with resignation to their impotence, or with a nominal revenge."

locality. They must take concerted actions to defend themselves—as by building dikes, relief measures, magical and religious activities. Moreover, the satisfactory exploitation of his land by an individual requires cooperation with others: similarly with the distribution of the produce and with trade and industry. The need of relaxation and amusement is another factor which will bring together individuals in games and other forms of group recreation. Thus the fact of living together and near to each other produces the need of political, economic, religious, and recreative organizations.

Prior to the arrival of the Japanese in Taiwan, villagers in Hsin Hsing (Gallin 1866) cultivated very little rice; instead they grew wheat, soybeans, sorghum, sweet potatoes, and similar dry land crops (pp. 14–16). This was not, then, an area of high potential for capital accumulation. In addition, the area was sparsely populated as late as the nineteenth century, and villagers lived in constant fear of bandits (p. 15). The village's small and weak agnatic groups (pp. 131–32) had good reasons, then, to play down agnatic differences. Access to land, water, and capital in Hsin Hsing does not depend on agnatic affiliation (pp. 92, 99, 101, 112, 113); and in many activities, especially irrigation, cooperation across agnatic lines is the rule (pp. 27–29, 49, 58–59, 64–68, 73–75, 176–79). As in Tatieh, economic cooperation between families is reflected in a variety of formal and informal associations. The total effect, as Gallin indicates, is that "such a diversity of activities with both relatives and nonrelatives in the village does have a tendency to undercut the solidarity of the *tsu* or kinship organizations. In addition, family activities and relationships, both kin and non-kin, also extend beyond the village" (p. 135).

Diamond makes a similar point about K'un Shen (1969: 75):

The people of K'un Shen put much stress on the importance of having friends. The routines of village life provide an opportunity to make a wide circle of acquaintances, if not close friends. Whereas the farmer may perform most of his work in the relative isolation of his own fields, fishermen see a great deal of each other during the day. In the afternoons, there are clusters of men seated at the beach, mending nets or waiting to go out to sea again. At certain seasons, several raft owners must come to an agreement to work together to encircle the fish—the partners chosen in these endeavors are usually described as "friends," though sometimes they may also be distant kinsmen. With over one-fourth of the village households belonging to one lineage, it is hard to avoid running into kinsmen. What is important is that it is more often friendship than kinship which forms the major bond between seasonal workmates.

Discussing undeveloped lineages among the Cantonese boat people of Hong Kong, Anderson (1970) underscores this supposed difference between fishermen and farmers. His argument seems to be that the boat people lack lineages because they have no land; all they have is a boat, which is "too small to hold very many people." The vast power of the lineage, on the other hand, is intimately linked to the paddy: "In southeast China, lineages flourish among the rice paddies, elite or no. But on the boats, lineages disappear, although Chinese culture remains unchanged."

What seems to me important, however, is not whether people have fields or boats, but whether their work requires or at least encourages cooperation between individuals and families on a basis that goes beyond kinship. Cooperation across agnatic lines is by no means adaptive only for fishermen—or even always for fishermen. Nor do all Chinese farmers work "in the relative isolation" of their own fields; how isolated they are depends on the type of crops grown, the distribution of fields, the nature of irrigation, and other variables. Farmers and fishermen alike cooperate in varying degrees not only to exploit natural resources, but in some cases to defend their access to these resources as well.

When all is said and done, two sets of more or less opposing behavior patterns, institutions, and beliefs can be found coexisting in all Chinese villages. One is in broad terms cooperative and aggregative; its effect is to weld a community together. The other is self-regarding and segmentary; its effect is to emphasize divisions and highlight distinctions. Which of these tendencies prevails, and to what extent, depends on circumstances, some of them immutable (e.g. origins, climate, soil), others subject to change (e.g. agricultural techniques, crops, government policy). A Chinese community is like a polyphony; its character depends on which voice conveys the theme. Other voices need not be silenced, however, and any of them may, when its time comes, rise to dominance.

References Cited

References Cited

Anderson, E. N. 1970. "Lineage Atrophy in Chinese Society," *American Anthropologist*, 72, no. 2: 363–65.

Baker, Hugh D. R. 1968. *A Chinese Lineage Village: Sheung Shui*. Stanford, Calif.: Stanford University Press.

Ballantine, Joseph W. 1952. *Formosa: A Problem for United States Foreign Policy*. Washington, D.C.: Brookings.

Barclay, George W. 1954. *Colonial Development and Population in Taiwan*. Princeton, N.J.: Princeton University Press.

Buck, John Lossing. 1956. *Land Utilization in China*. New York: Council on Economic and Cultural Affairs.

Chang Fen-ch'ien. 1960. *K'o-chia Min-feng Min-su Chih Yen-chiu* (Researches on popular Hakka customs). Taipei: T'ai-ching Ch'u-pan She.

———— 1962. "K'o-chia Min-hsi Chih Yen-hua" (On Hakka transition and growth), *Taiwan Wen Shian*, 13: 49–87.

Chang Yen-tien. 1954. *Land Reform in Taiwan*. Taichung: Department of Agricultural Economics, Taiwan Provincial College of Agriculture.

Chen Cheng. 1961. *Land Reform in Taiwan*. Taiwan: China Publishing Co.

Chen Cheng-siang. 1960. *T'ai-wan Ti-chih* (A geography of Taiwan), vol. 2. Taipei: Research Report No. 94, Fu-min Geographical Institute of Economic Development.

———— 1963. *Taiwan: An Economic and Social Geography*, vol. 1. Taipei: Research Report No. 96, Fu-min Geographical Institute of Economic Development.

Ch'en Ch'i-lu. 1967. "A Brief History of Taiwan," *Journal of the China Society*, 5: 77–91.

Chen Shao-hsing. 1956. "Social Change in Taiwan," *Studia Taiwanica*, no. 1: 1–19.

Chuang Chin-teh. 1964. "Ch'ing-ch'u Yen-chin Yen-hai Jen-min T'ou-tu Lai-t'ai Shih-mo" (An account of early Ch'ing prohibitions on the immigrations of coastal peoples to Taiwan), *Taiwan Wen Shian*, 15, no. 3: 1–20; and 15, no. 4: 40–62.

Chung Jen-shou. n.d. *Liu-tui Hsiang-t'u K'ai-fa Shih* (History of the Liu-tui). Liu-tui Hsiang T'u-chih Chu-pien.

Cohen, Myron L. 1967. "Variations in Complexity Among Chinese Family Groups: The Impact of Modernization," *Transactions of the New York Academy of Sciences*, ser. II, vol. 29, no. 5: 638–44.

———— 1968. "The Hakka or 'Guest People': Dialect as a Sociocultural Variable in Southeastern China," *Ethnohistory*, 15, no. 3: 237–92.

———— 1969. "Agnatic Kinship in South Taiwan," *Ethnology*, 8, no. 2: 167–82.

———— 1970. "Developmental Process in the Chinese Domestic Group," in Maurice Freedman, ed., *Family and Kinship in Chinese Society*. Stanford, Calif.: Stanford University Press, pp. 21–36.

D'Estrey, Comte Meyners. 1890. "Les Hakka et les Hoklo, L'autonomie des villages en Chine," *Revue de geographie*, 27: 29–35, 95–103.

Diamond, Norma. 1969. *K'un Shen: A Taiwan Village*. New York: Holt, Rinehart & Winston.

Eberhard, Wolfram. 1962. *Social Mobility in Traditional China*. Leiden.

Fei Hsiao-tung. 1939. *Peasant Life in China*. London: Routledge.

Freedman, Maurice. 1957. *Chinese Family and Marriage in Singapore*. London: Colonial Research Studies, No. 20.

———— 1958. *Lineage Organization in Southeastern China*. London: Athlone.

———— 1966. *Chinese Lineage and Society: Fukien and Kwangtung*. New York: Humanities Press.

———— 1970. "Ritual Aspects of Chinese Kinship and Marriage," in Maurice Freedman, ed., *Family and Kinship in Chinese Society*. Stanford, Calif.: Stanford University Press, pp. 163–87.

Fried, Morton H. 1953. *Fabric of Chinese Society*. New York: Praeger.

———— 1957. "The Classification of Corporate Unilineal Descent Groups," *Journal of the Royal Anthropological Institute*, 87: 1–29.

———— 1966. "Some Political Aspects of Clanship in a Modern Chinese City," in Marc J. Swartz, Victor W. Turner, and Arthur Tuden, eds., *Political Anthropology*. Chicago: Aldine, pp. 285–300.

Gallin, Bernard. 1960. "Matrilateral and Affinal Relationships of a Taiwanese Village," *American Anthropologist*, 62: 632–42.

———— 1963. "Land Reform in Taiwan: Its Effect on Rural Social Organization and Leadership," *Human Organization*, 22: no. 2: 109–12.

———— 1966. *Hsin Hsing, Taiwan: A Chinese Village in Change*. Berkeley: University of California Press.

General Report on the 1961 Census of Agriculture, Taiwan, Republic of China. 1963. Committee on Census of Agriculture, Taiwan Provincial Government.

Hsiao Kung-chuan. 1960. *Rural China: Imperial Control in the Nineteenth Century*. Seattle: University of Washington Press.

Hsieh, T'ing-yu. 1929. "Origin and Migrations of the Hakkas," *The Chinese Social and Political Science Review*, 13: 202–27.

Hu Hsien-chin. 1948. *The Common Descent Group in China and Its Functions*. New York: Viking Fund, Publications in Anthropology, No. 10.

Jones, Lewis W. 1955. "The Hinterland Reconsidered," *American Sociological Review*, 20: 40–44.

Kuang-hsü Chia-ying Chou-chih (The Kuang-hsü gazetteer of Chiaying Chou). 1961. Taipei: Mei-hsien T'ung-hsiang Hui (Republication of 1903 gazetteer).

Kulp, D. H. 1925. *Country Life in South China*. New York: Teachers College, Columbia University Bureau of Publications.

Kuo-shih T'iao-ch'a Chieh-kuo Piao 1935 (National situation investigation results for 1935). 1937. Taipei: Government-General of Taiwan, Bureau of Official Statistics.

Kuo Shou-hua. 1963. *K'o-chia Yüan-liu Hsin-chih* (New record of the origins and history of the Hakka). Taipei: published by the author.

Lang, Olga. 1946. *Chinese Family and Society*. New Haven: Yale University Press.

Lin Yueh-hwa. 1948. *The Golden Wing: A Sociological Study of Chinese Familism*. New York: Oxford University Press.

Liu Chao-shu. n.d. "T-ai-wan Kao-p'ing Erh-hsien K'o-chia I-wang K'ao" (Researches on the migrations of Hakka in Kaohsiung and Pingtung counties). Unpublished manuscript, copy of which is in my possession.

Orenstein, Henry. 1956. "Irrigation, Settlement Pattern, and Social Organization," in *Selected Papers of the Fifth International Congress of Anthropological and Ethnological Sciences*. Philadelphia: University of Pennsylvania Press, pp. 318–23.

———— 1965. "Notes on the Ecology of Irrigation Agriculture in Contemporary Peasant Societies," *American Anthropologist*, 67: 1529–32.

Pasternak, Burton. 1968a. "Agnatic Atrophy in a Formosan Village," *American Anthropologist*, 70: 93–96.

———— 1968b. "Atrophy of Patrilineal Bonds in a Chinese Village in Historical Perspective," *Ethnohistory*, 15, no. 3: 293–327.

———— 1968c. "On the Social Consequences of Equalizing Irrigation Access," *Human Organization*, 27, no. 4: 332–43.

———— 1968d. "Some Social Consequences of Land Reform in a Taiwanese Village," *Eastern Anthropologist*, 28, no. 3: 551–61.

———— 1972. "The Sociology of Irrigation: Two Taiwanese Villages," in W. E. Willmott, ed., *Economic Organization in Chinese Society*. Stanford, Calif.: Stanford University Press, pp. 193–213.

Paton, Bernard W. n.d. *The "Stranger People," a Story and a Challenge*. London: Religious Tract Society.

Potter, Jack M. 1968. *Capitalism and the Chinese Peasant*. Berkeley: University of California Press.

———— 1970. "Land and Lineage in Traditional China," in Maurice Freedman, ed., *Family and Kinship in Chinese Society*. Stanford, Calif.: Stanford University Press, pp. 121–38.

Pratt, Jean A. 1960. "Emigration and Unilineal Descent Groups: A Study of Marriage in a Hakka Village in the New Territories, Hong Kong," *Eastern Anthropologist*, 13: 147–58.

Report on the 1964 Irrigated Land Survey of Irrigation Associations in Taiwan, The Republic of China. 1965. Taipei: Provincial Water Conservancy Bureau.

Sahlins, Marshall D. 1961. "The Segmentary Lineage: An Organization of Predatory Expansion," *American Anthropologist*, 63: 322–45.

Service, Elman. 1962. *Primitive Social Organization: An Evolutionary Perspective.* New York: Random House.

Soils and Fertilizer Uses in Taiwan, Republic of China. 1961. Taipei: JCRR, Plant Industry Series, No. 20.

Ta Chen. 1923. *Chinese Migrations, with Special Reference to Labor Conditions.* Washington, D.C.

T'ai-wan Sheng Miao-li Hsien-chih (The gazetteer of Miaoli county in Taiwan province). 1960.

Taiwan Agricultural Yearbook. 1964. Department of Agriculture and Forestry, Provincial Government of Taiwan.

Tawney, R. H. 1966. *Land and Labor in China.* Boston: Beacon Press (originally published in 1932).

Tsui, Y. C. 1959. *A Summary Report on Farm Income of Taiwan in 1957 in Comparison with 1952.* Taipei: JCRR Economic Digest Series, No. 13.

Wan-luan Hsiang-chih Ch'u-kao (First draft of the Wanluan township gazetteer). 1971. Wanluan Township Office.

Wiens, Herold J. 1954. *China's March Toward the Tropics.* Hamden: Shoe String Press.

Wittfogel, Karl A. 1935. "The Foundations and Stages of Chinese Economic History," *Zeitschrift für Sozialforsdrung*, 4, 4.

——— 1938. *New Light on Chinese Society: An Investigation of China's Socio-Economic Structure.* New York: International Secretariat, Institute of Pacific Relations.

Yang, C. K. 1959a. *The Chinese Family in the Communist Revolution.* Cambridge: Massachusetts Institute of Technology, Technology Press.

——— 1959b. *A Chinese Village in Early Communist Transition.* Cambridge: Massachusetts Institute of Technology, Technology Press.

Yang, Martin. 1948. *A Chinese Village.* London: Kegan Paul, Trench, Trubner.

Index

Index

aborigines, 5, 13, 102f, 142, 146, 148, 154

accountant, village, 113–14

adoption, 2, 60, 66–67, 84–85, 91, 93–94

Advanced Age Society, 108

affinal ties, 56, 61–67 *passim*, 72, 81–84 *passim*, 132–33, 139; and membership in corporate associations, 102, 121, 124

aggregation, 152–53, 159

agnatic affiliation (patrilineal affiliation), 14–15, 38, 60–61, 72–77 *passim*, 136, 146, 148, 155; agnatic groups, 1, 18f, 86, 128, 140, 149, 150; emphasis on, in Chungshe, 1f, 61, 82; and village factionalism, 2, 99, 105, 107, 116–18; and village residential patterns, 6f, 56, 121; and access to agricultural resources, 20–25 *passim*, 36–37, 38, 42, 56, 77; and lending practices, 35–36, 57; Hakka emphasis on, 62, 133–34; and ceremonial occasions, 63–66 *passim*, 82ff, 109, 111, 113; and adoption practices, 67, 84–85; and village administration, 96–100 *passim*, 114; and membership in corporate associations, 102, 120, 122, 124. *See also* descent groups; family; lineages; surname groups

agriculture, *see* climate; crops; irrigation; land; mechanization; resources, agricultural; tenant farming; water

ancestor worship, 7, 14, 63, 71–76 *passim*, 83, 89, 91, 109, 132f; during

festivals, 110f, 113, 127. *See also* religion; rituals

ancestral estates (ancestral trusts), 75–76, 87–94 *passim*, 134, 137–38, 154, 155n

ancestral hall, 7, 14, 71–75 *passim*, 83, 91

ancestral tablets, 7, 14, 71, 76, 83, 89, 91. *See also* ancestor worship

ancestral trusts, *see* ancestral estates

Anderson, E. N., 159

associations, corporate, *see* corporate associations

associations, cross-kin, *see* corporate associations

Baker, Hugh D. R., 157

bananas, 8, 24, 35, 101

bandits, 118–23 *passim*, 142–48 *passim*, 155, 158

Barclay, George W., 130

betel nuts, 8

birthdays, celebration of, 61, 64, 82f, 108f

Buck, John Lossing, 53

Buddha Society, 122, 125

buffalo, 33–34, 42, 49

Canton, 129

Cantonese, 133, 151n, 152, 153n, 159

capital, access to, 20, 22, 34–36, 56–57, 61, 158

ceremonial behavior, 2, 61–66 *passim*, 72ff, 82–84, 93–94, 95, 109–14, 122–27 *passim*, 134. *See also* feasts; religion, rituals